dog care essentials

dog care essentials

hamlyn **all color**

Everything you need to know at a glance

Caroline Davis

hamlyn

An Hachette UK Company
www.hachette.co.uk

First published in Great Britain in 2010 by
Hamlyn, a division of Octopus Publishing Group Ltd
Endeavour House
189 Shaftesbury Avenue
London
WC2H 8JY
www.octopusbooksusa.com

Distributed in the U.S. and Canada by Octopus Books
USA:
c/o Hachette Book Group
237 Park Avenue
New York, NY 10017

ISBN 978-0-600-62093-8

Printed and bound in China

10 9 8 7 6 5 4 3 2 1

Note
Unless the information is specific to males or females,
throughout this book dogs are referred to as 'he' and
the information and advice are applicable to both sexes.

The advice in this book is provided as general
information only. It is not necessarily specific to any
individual case and is not a substitute for the guidance
and advice provided by a licensed veterinary practitioner
consulted in any particular situation. Octopus Publishing
Group accepts no liability or responsibility for any
consequences resulting from the use of or reliance upon
the information contained herein.

No dogs were harmed in the making of this book.

Contents

Introduction **6**

Quick dog facts **8**

The canine body **20**

Puppy care **42**

Growing up **58**

Routine care **72**

Fitness and food **88**

Simple training solutions **98**

Problem behaviours **130**

Out and about **148**

Health care **154**

The senior dog **172**

Index **188**

Acknowledgements **192**

Introduction

Congratulations! You are thinking of getting a dog, and there's no better friend a person could have. A dog is loyal, affectionate, full of fun and a sincere and faithful companion, come rain or shine. And if you are feeling a bit down, or have no one to turn to for comfort when needed, your dog is always there to lend a sympathetic ear and a steadfast and warm, furry, shoulder to lean on. Just getting out of the house to take him for a walk will also help blow the cobwebs away, relieve your stress and is physically good for you, too.

In return for providing you with these benefits, all that your dog requires is to be kept comfortable, healthy and happy. To do this, you need to know a dog's requirements in terms of sustenance and attention, daily care, such as grooming and exercise, training – so he doesn't get himself and you into bother – and, most of all, your understanding of how he 'ticks' so that you can communicate in order to have a richly rewarding relationship and life together.

Whether you are new to dog ownership – or indeed have one already – no doubt you'll have lots of questions as regards looking after your four-legged canine friend. For instance: How can I tell if he's hungry and thirsty? What's he trying to say to me? When do I need to call a vet? Where can I find a

dog trainer or look for advice if I have a behavioural problem with my dog?

With many of us leading busy lives these days, the last thing you may have time for is trawling through countless dog books, magazines or Internet searches looking for the answers, so this at-a-glance guide is designed to cover your key questions about dog ownership from start to finish, quickly and simply. If you need more in-depth information on a subject, this book will point you in the right direction on where to look or whom to ask for advice.

So, if you are looking for the easiest way to solve a canine conundrum, this book is the essential quick-reference guide for you. Happy dog-owning!

Quick dog facts

Dogs are popular pets worldwide and have been man's best friend for centuries. Whether pedigree or mongrel, large or small, there's sure to be a dog out there to suit you and your lifestyle. Here are a few quick pointers to help you choose a pet that will bring you a lifetime of affection and companionship.

Dogs are good for you!

Dogs make wonderful companions for humans, with key requirements from their owners being unconditional affection and loyalty from their pet. But did you know that there are also many health benefits to having a dog, or at least access to one? It's true – as recent research studies have proved.

Education – research by Warwick University has shown that children who are brought up with a dog do better at school, are less likely to take days off sick, are more relaxed and confident and have a healthier respect for their fellow creatures.

Stress relief – stroking dogs has been proven to have a beneficial effect on the blood pressure of the human doing the stroking. Just a few minutes sitting quietly and petting your dog can do wonders for lowering your stress or anxiety levels and making you feel happy, calm and relaxed. And your dog enjoys it, too.

Key fact
Dog owners walk an average 44 minutes more per week than non-owners.

Feel-good factor – because dogs help to make you feel happy, this helps to boost your immune system.

Mind and body fitness – independent research from around the world compiled by Dogs Trust (a UK canine charity) showed that dog owners make fewer annual doctor visits and spend less time in hospital than non-owners. Walking a dog on a daily basis helps keep your cardiovascular system fit, and your body at the ideal weight, toned and supple.

Carers and companions – dogs help alleviate depression and loneliness in humans, as well as assist their recovery from medical conditions, such as heart attacks.

Development issues – it's been found that children with social and learning difficulties have improved through having contact with dogs.

Dogs and children

Dogs make wonderful companions, confidantes and playmates for children (see pages 10–11) – providing both are taught how to behave around each other and what their boundaries are. Once ground rules are established, and adhered to, they're bound to be lifelong pals who'll have great fun together.

Respect – teach children to respect dogs by treating them kindly, consistently, patiently and quietly. Show them how to gently stroke, handle and talk to dogs. Never let them tease a dog, or retaliation/self-preservation may come in the form of a bite.

Interaction – involve children in your dog's daily care routine, walks, playtime and training sessions. Grooming your pet together helps bonding and is pleasurable for all concerned (see pages 80–81 for some grooming tips).

Carrying – don't let young children pick up and carry a dog without supervision. Children tend to clutch on to and squeeze dogs, as they would a toy, which may distress the pet. Plus there's the risk of youngsters tripping and falling with the dog. Show older children how to safely pick up and carry a puppy or small dog (see pages 54–55).

No staring – children like to stare at things and study them, but dogs do not like to be stared at and may consider such action a threat. Teach children not to stare at dogs, and to avoid direct, prolonged eye contact.

Rough play – it's essential that children do not encourage dogs to get over-exuberant during play as dogs can become rough in excitement and end up unintentionally nipping or pushing children over. Keep play low-key.

Key question
At what age can children be left alone with a dog?

For safety's sake, never leave young children alone with a dog of any age, no matter how quiet and amenable he is. Supervise all interaction until the child is at least 12 years old and can be considered responsible and disciplined.

Choosing a dog

Thinking about getting a dog is exciting. There are so many different breeds, types, colours, shapes and sizes that it can make choosing just one quite hard. The chances are that you'll already have an idea of what type you want, but do consider whether your lifestyle, home facilities and pet-available time will suit him.

Homework – first of all, having taken into account your lifestyle, decide what sort of dog would fulfil your requirements – big, small, longhaired, shorthaired, and so forth.

Online information – search the Internet for a wealth of information on breeds, types and breed clubs around the world. Specialist books on breeds and types, too, are an excellent source of gleaning knowledge.

Hair and slobber – if you are house-proud, then a big dog that sheds hair and drools strings of saliva will probably not suit you.

BRIEF BREED CHARACTERISTICS

Group or type	Characteristics
Working and guarding breeds	Can be quite demanding and strong-willed
Herding breeds	Intelligent and sensitive
Hounds	Affectionate but independent
Gundogs	Tend to be good-natured and quick to learn
Terriers	Often determined and vocal
Toy breeds	Usually friendly and affectionate
Cross-breeds and mongrels	Generally quite hardy and friendly

Things to consider

- **Size** – ensure that your home will accommodate him
- **Grooming requirements** – can you cope with his coat care?
- **Exercise needs** – you must be able and have time to exercise a dog
- **Feeding requirements** – ensure that you are able to afford food costs
- **Health issues** – check if a breed you like is prone to particular ailments and invest in the most comprehensive insurance cover you can afford
- **Family friendly** – pick a breed/type known to love people
- **Pet compatible** – choose a type likely to get on with other household pets

Puppies look cute when small, but check what characteristics they are likely to have when mature.

Types – pedigrees are not necessarily more loving, clever or naughty than mongrels. It's more usually how you bring up, handle and train a dog that determines how biddable and amenable he will turn out to be.

Allergy sufferers – some people with allergies say that certain breeds are easier to live with than others – such as Poodles, hairless dogs and the Bichon Frise – but that is not always the case due to allergens in canine urine, saliva and dander (skin flakes). It is advisable for allergy sufferers to speak to their doctor about any health risks involved.

Normal canine behaviour

Dogs do many things that humans may find strange, or even disgusting sometimes, but once you understand why they do it, such behaviour can be more acceptable to us and we learn to live with, or control, it in such a way that doesn't distress a dog.

Drinking dirty water – dogs often take a drink from dirty puddles and slimy ponds, but then their sense of taste is not as keen as ours. Avoid letting him do so since the water could be polluted or harbour parasites.

Sniffing bottoms – dogs sniff each other, particularly around the anus, to identify each

other and check out sexual status. They do the same to humans, too, for the same reason – and some dogs are more persistent at this than others, but can be trained not to by teaching him the command 'No' or 'Leave' (see pages 118–119).

Grass-scratching – scratching up grass with the front and back legs after urinating and defecating is a way of marking territory via scent glands in the feet; it's also thought to be a sign of relief after toileting. Turn to pages 36–39 for more on canine behaviour and communication.

Digging – this is a perfectly normal thing for a dog to do so, if needs be, create his own burrowing area in your garden.

Eating faeces – some dogs do this, as other animals' droppings contain nutrients that appeal to a dog. However, try not to let him eat faeces since they could contain parasites or medication.

'Scooting' – when a dogs drags his bottom on the floor it indicates he has a problem in his anal region, which could be due to worms, blocked anal glands, constipation or soreness. Take him to a vet to determine the cause and obtain appropriate treatment.

Key question
Why does my dog roll in other animals' faeces? He smells so bad afterwards.
Rolling in faeces (or on dead animals and birds) is a dog's natural instinct to mask his own scent in preparation for hunting. However, this behaviour is not to be encouraged (see pages 82–83 on bathing).

Rescue dogs

Puppies and adult dogs end up in rescue centres for many reasons, often through unfortunate circumstance and no fault of their own. In some cases, owners have not wanted to give up their dog, but had no choice. You can help reduce the population of homeless dogs by offering one of them a home.

Start right – giving a caring home to a rescue dog is a satisfying feeling, but remember that he should not be allowed to get away with bad behaviour just because 'he's a rescue dog'. He'll need appropriate handling and, possibly training, like any other dog.

Rescue centres – have a mixed selection of dogs of all ages, so you can see many types under one roof. Rescue dogs are often neutered, vaccinated and microchipped before being rehomed. You will have to pass an owner suitability check in most cases before a centre will rehome a dog with you. A sizeable donation is usually required.

Breed rescue – if you are looking for a particular breed, then breed clubs usually operate a breed rescue service to match unwanted dogs with new owners.

Old dogs – potential owners often overlook aged dogs in favour of younger dogs. Golden oldies, however, have so much affection and loyalty to give, are often trained and can have many years of life and good health left in them.

Incompatibility – sometimes a dog just doesn't settle into his new environment, or proves unsuitable due to previously unknown behaviour traits for his new owners, despite efforts to the contrary. In these cases, contact where you got him from for advice and possibly return him in extreme cases.

The canine body

All dogs, whatever their breed, share the same physiology (the way in which a living creature functions); they differ only in minor ways to produce a larger, smaller, more compact or elongated conformation, with some displaying anomalies of fur, balance, physical advantages or limitations, or bone structure caused by particular mutations or selective breeding.

The canine skeleton

Dogs have a skeleton that shelters their internal organs and supports skin, enabling them to procure and process food and water to live, and to reproduce in order for the species to survive. On average, the skeleton comprises 320 bones and the key canine skeletal facts are described below.

Skeleton – a semi-rigid framework that's constructed to enable a dog to move at speed, chase and hunt. The axial skeleton comprises the skull, vertebral column, ribs and sternum, while the appendicular skeleton consists of limb bones and supporting thoracic and pelvic girdles. During foetal development, body cells gradually form to create an outline framework of cartilage and connective tissue, then ossification (bone formation) takes place to create a firm skeleton.

Bones – the size and shape of bones varies depending on the breed and type of dog. A system of efficient levers to aid movement comprises the bones of the spine, limbs, shoulders and pelvis, working together with muscles, ligaments and tendons.

Protection – the skull, ribcage and pelvis protect the major organs they contain comprising the brain, heart and lungs, intestines, kidneys and reproductive organs.

Four key bones – these make up the skeleton: the long (limb bones), short (feet bones and patella), irregular (spine and tail bones) and flat bones (skull, pelvis, shoulder blades and ribs).

Skull shape – there are three terms used to describe skull shape: mesaticephalic – average shape, such as in the Labrador Retriever; dolichoephalic – long and narrow, such as in the Greyhound; and brachycephalic – short and wide, such as in the Bulldog.

Feet – there are four toes and nails on each foot (paws), and a fifth toe (dewclaw) that serves no useful purpose, although certain breeds don't have dewclaws while others, such as the Briard, sport double dewclaws on the rear lower legs (pasterns).

Key facts

With over 200 breeds of dog, there is a greater range of size and shape in canine heads than in any other mammalian species.

The head is also large compared to other mammals due to it housing a large brain and well developed sensory organs.

THE SKELETON

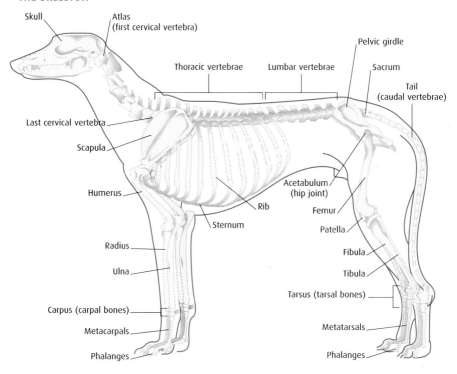

Skull

Atlas
(first cervical vertebra)

Pelvic girdle

Thoracic vertebrae

Lumbar vertebrae

Sacrum

Tail
(caudal vertebrae)

Last cervical vertebra

Scapula

Humerus

Acetabulum
(hip joint)

Rib

Femur

Sternum

Patella

Radius

Fibula

Ulna

Tibula

Tarsus (tarsal bones)

Carpus (carpal bones)

Metacarpals

Metatarsals

Phalanges

Phalanges

The muscular system

Overlying the skeletal framework is a complex network of muscles that enables a dog's movement, and also move substances such as food and blood through the body. Muscle tissue is made up of cells that can shorten and lengthen to produce a voluntary or involuntary action. There are three types of muscle – skeletal (also called striped or striated); visceral (smooth or unstriated); and cardiac.

Skeletal muscles – these are mainly attached to limbs and other parts of the anatomy that are under the voluntary control of the dog, such as movement, and are also known as voluntary muscles. They form the flesh (meat) of the dog and are attached to bones in order to produce movement.

Visceral muscles – these automatically carry out muscular functions not under the dog's voluntary control, such as muscles of the intestines and walls of blood vessels, so they are known as involuntary muscles. They are not as strong as skeletal muscles but their contractions last longer.

Key questions
How are muscles attached to bones and what keeps bones together?
Flexible but inelastic cords of fibrous tissue called tendons attach muscle to bone, while ligaments – short bands of tough, fibrous connective tissue – connect bones or cartilages and hold joints together. Ligaments also comprise membranous folds that support organs and keep them in position.

Can a dog pull a muscle?
Yes, in the way that humans can through undue exertion, especially when suddenly energetic before muscles have warmed up through gentle exercise first. Ask your vet as to the best way of treating the injury.

THE MUSCLES

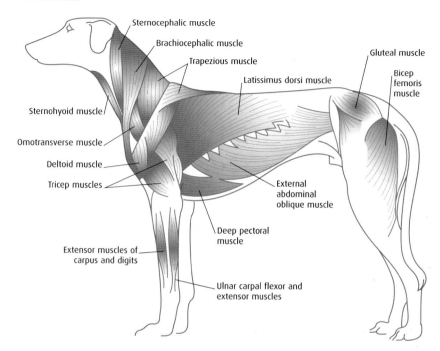

Sternocephalic muscle

Brachiocephalic muscle

Trapezious muscle

Latissimus dorsi muscle

Gluteal muscle

Bicep femoris muscle

Sternohyoid muscle

Omotransverse muscle

Deltoid muscle

Tricep muscles

External abdominal oblique muscle

Deep pectoral muscle

Extensor muscles of carpus and digits

Ulnar carpal flexor and extensor muscles

Cardiac muscle – this is confined to the heart and carries out powerful and rhythmic contractions to pump blood around the body.

Function categories – extensor muscles extend and straighten a limb. Flexor muscles flex and bend joints. Abductor muscles move limbs away from the body and adductor muscles move them back in again.

Movement – a muscle does not usually produce an action on its own, but works as part of a group of muscles, and can only action movement when it contracts. Muscles also work to check quick movement in order that the ligaments that reinforce joints are not damaged.

The respiratory system

Respiration provides the dog's body with the oxygen that is vital for life, and expels waste products in the form of nitrogen and carbon dioxide gases from the blood. Oxygen is carried around the body via the blood, enabling body cells to live and be renewed so that the dog can function.

Air passage – oxygen enters the dog's body when he inhales through his nostrils and mouth, then it goes down the trachea (windpipe) and into the lungs. Waste gases exit the body via the same route in reverse when the dog exhales.

Key questions

Is it normal for a dog to wheeze when breathing or should I be concerned?

Wheezing, or other abnormal sounds, when breathing indicate that something is wrong and should be investigated by a vet. Some overly exaggerated-type dogs in brachycephalic breeds (see opposite) are prone to breathing problems where the length of the nose is extremely short and nostrils are tiny.

Trachea – the trachea is a flexible, hollow tube comprising 35 ring-shaped tracheal cartilages that prevent the tube from collapsing. To stop food, water and other objects (such as stones and toys) entering it via the mouth, and getting into the lungs, a valve called the larynx guards the entrance.

Respiration rate – how many times a dog inhales and exhales a minute depends on his size, age, environment and body temperature, general health and emotional state. Generally, a normal respiration rate is 10–30 breaths in 60 seconds. Small and young puppies breathe faster.

Brachycephalic breeds – (see pages 22–23) such as Shih Tzus, Bulldogs and others with 'squashed' faces, wheeze in their efforts to draw in enough oxygen due to tiny nostrils and restricted, short nasal passages limiting their air intake.

Key fact

Panting helps keep dogs cool. Drawing cold air in over the tongue and passing it out again reduces body heat by water evaporation from the tongue, lips, mouth cavity and lungs. However, dogs are prone to overheating, which is why they should never be left unattended in vehicles on warm days – many dogs die every year because of this.

THE RESPIRATORY SYSTEM

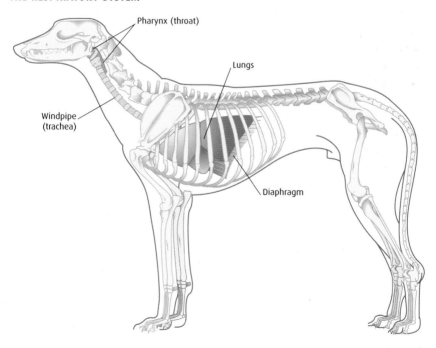

Pharynx (throat)

Lungs

Windpipe (trachea)

Diaphragm

The circulatory system

Every cell in a dog's body needs nourishment and this is delivered via the blood, which also removes waste products from the body. Blood is continually pumped around the body by the heart, which is at the centre of the circulatory system and housed for protection within the rib cage.

Key question
What is a normal pulse rate?

Your dog's pulse rate will depend on his size and weight. Take his pulse rate when he is healthy and relaxed (see page 159) so that you know what is normal for your particular dog, use the table below as a guide. Large dogs tend to have slower heart rates. The fitter a healthy dog is, the slower his heart rate will be at rest compared to unfit dogs of similar size, type and weight.

Size	Average pulse rate
Under 12 months	120–180 bpm
Toy	120–180 bpm
Small	90–160 bpm
Medium	70–110 bpm
Large	60–90 bpm

Blood components – blood is made up of red blood cells and white blood corpuscles that are contained in a fluid called plasma. Plasma contains platelets that in turn contain a blood-clotting agent in the event of superficial cuts and wounds.

Pumping action – blood pumped by the heart through the aorta causes its walls to expand and a pressure wave to pass down the arteries – this is known as the pulse. For normal pulse rate, see left.

Vital roles – red blood cells carry oxygen and nutrients derived from food, while white blood corpuscles vacuum up and transport impurities and bacteria that have invaded red cells.

Delivering 'goodies' – oxygen-rich blood is pumped from the heart into the aorta to run quickly through all other arteries, distributing its store of oxygen collected from the lungs and

THE CIRCULATORY SYSTEM

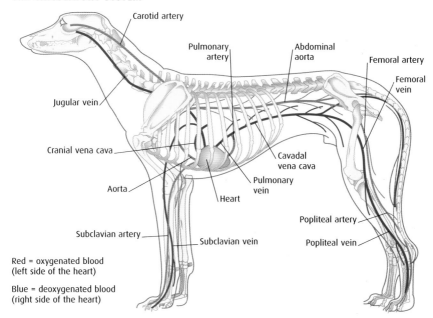

Carotid artery

Pulmonary artery

Abdominal aorta

Femoral artery

Femoral vein

Jugular vein

Cranial vena cava

Cavadal vena cava

Aorta

Pulmonary vein

Heart

Subclavian artery

Subclavian vein

Popliteal artery

Popliteal vein

Red = oxygenated blood
(left side of the heart)

Blue = deoxygenated blood
(right side of the heart)

nutrients gathered from the small intestine.
Blood also collects waste matter comprising
bacteria, dead blood cells and carbon dioxide.

Removing rubbish – laden with waste
products, blood then enters veins on its
slower way back to the heart, dumping its
rubbish at appropriate points to be expelled
from the body. When it gets back to the
lungs, it is replenished with oxygen before
starting its journey all over again.

Key fact

The amount of blood in a dog's body
varies depending on size, but research
states that the average circulating blood
volume is 66 ml per kilogram of body-
weight. For blood transfusions, one
canine unit of blood is 450 ml (16 fl oz),
which could safely be taken from a
healthy 25 kg (55 lb) canine donor.

The digestive system

Keeping your dog's digestive system in optimum working order is essential for health. Providing a good diet and fresh water will fuel his activities and keep him alert, fit and happy. The more digestible the food, the less waste in the form of faeces is produced.

Omnivores – although they are commonly thought to be carnivorous, dogs, whatever the breed, are actually omnivorous, which means they can eat both meat and plant material to get enough protein and other nutrients to survive.

Lips and tongue – large and muscular, the tongue is covered in taste buds that can detect bitter, salty, sour and sweet tastes (see page 35). It laps up fluids and licks up food particles. Lips serve to keep food and liquid in the mouth until it is swallowed.

Teeth – dogs usually have a total of 42 – 20 in the upper jaw and 22 in the lower, comprising 4 canines, 12 incisors, 12 molars and 14 premolars. Canines are used to stab, rip and hold; incisors for cutting, nipping, nibbling (gnawing) and grasping; and molars and premolars for carrying, shearing and chewing. Milk teeth in puppies are replaced by permanent teeth at around six months of age.

Mastication – although dogs have an impressive array of teeth, they don't tend to chew food up as humans do before swallowing it, but gobble it down quickly.

Saliva – this is produced in the mouth via glands, and helps to ease food passage down the oesophagus (gullet) into the stomach where it is broken up into chyme

Key question
Why do dogs eat grass and then vomit it back up?
Dogs eat grass as an aid to cleansing the stomach. The tickly grass acts as an irritant when swallowed, making the dog vomit up stomach contents.

(a soupy mixture of partly digested food and gastric juices).

Digestion – chyme passes into the small intestine where nutrients – fats, sugars, minerals, vitamins, proteins and carbohydrates – are extracted. The liver neutralizes toxins. Remaining matter passes into the large intestine where excess fluid is removed via the kidneys and bladder as urine, while solid matter moves on into the rectum to be expelled through the anus as faeces. Faeces should be neither too hard not sloppy, both of these consistencies indicate a digestive problem which, if it does not clear up swiftly, should be investigated by a vet.

THE DIGESTIVE SYSTEM

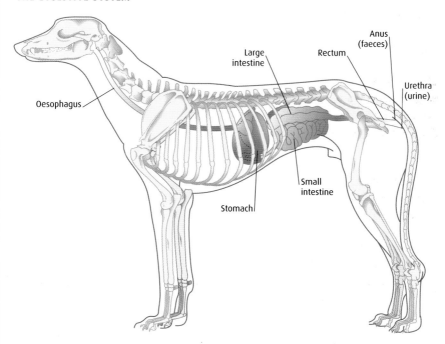

Oesophagus

Large intestine

Rectum

Anus (faeces)

Urethra (urine)

Stomach

Small intestine

A healthy coat

The canine coat isn't just pleasant to stroke and appealing to look at, thus helping the human-canine bond, it has essential protection, insulation and water-proofing qualities, too. The skin, which the coat is attached to, also provides vital functions and is the largest sensory organ in the dog's body.

Skin – three thin layers of tissue (epidermis, dermis and fatty hypodermis) comprise strong and elastic skin to keep out foreign bodies, retain moisture, protect inner structures, regulate body temperature and manufacture vital vitamin D. Nerve endings in the skin function as receptors for pain, pressure and temperature.

Glands – in the skin glands help to expel waste products from the body. Dogs do not sweat through skin glands, apart from a few in the feet, so they help cool themselves down by drawing in cool air through the mouth (panting). Feet glands leave an identifying, individual scent. The coat's silky oiliness is maintained by fatty secretions from secretary (sebaceous) glands.

Key fact

In healthy dogs, the skin is pliable; in sick dogs, it is stiff and unyielding. A change from the normal pale pink colouring, especially in the lips and gums, can indicate illness: white indicates anaemia; inflammation is signified by reddening; blue indicates circulatory trouble, respiratory disease or poisoning; yellow is a sign of liver dysfunction.

Hairs – the double coat of longhaired breeds, such as German Shepherd dogs and Golden Retrievers, has two types of hair (top coat and undercoat). Guard (primary; top coat), hairs are strong, and may be straight, wavy or tightly curled. They repel water and protect the finer, insulating, vellus (wool hairs; undercoat). Single-coated breeds, for example Greyhounds, have fewer or no vellus hairs and can easily become cold. In colder weather these dogs may need coats for outdoor exercise.

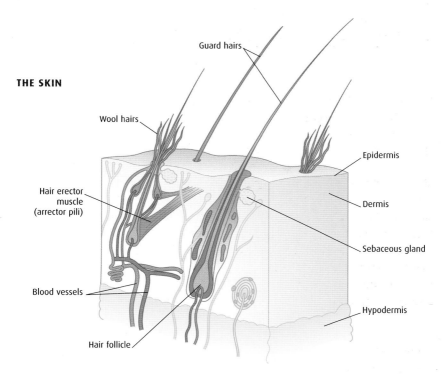

THE SKIN

Guard hairs

Wool hairs

Epidermis

Hair erector muscle (arrector pili)

Dermis

Sebaceous gland

Blood vessels

Hypodermis

Hair follicle

Whiskers – these are sensory hairs (vibrissae) that are thick and sited on the head. Sensitive to touch, they help a dog prevent bumping into things. Canine whiskers work in a similar way to cats' whiskers, in that dogs, too, use them as a gauge to judge if they can fit into narrow spaces, and to feel their way around – especially in the dark. Whiskers also detect vibration and movement nearby.

Shedding (moulting) – hair is shed more during spring and autumn to make way for summer and winter coats, though some breeds and those dogs living indoors may shed continuously. Continual moulting is usually a result of central heating (along with warmer climates), to help prevent the dog overheating. It can also be due to a lack of omega-3 and -6 oils. Changes in coat appearance can be symptomatic of disease.

Canine senses

A dog perceives his surroundings through his five vital bodily senses – sight, hearing, smell, taste and touch. Dogs predominantly use their noses and mouths to find out about their world, whereas humans use their eyes and hands. Eyes and ears are important communication tools, too, for our canine companions.

Hearing – a dog's keen hearing is vastly superior to a human's as it is up to 10 times more sensitive to sounds than we are – especially those at high frequencies, which we cannot hear. Mobile ears help pinpoint sound sources since they can be directed to it.

Smell – canines have an exceptional sense of smell: it is essential for his sex life, detecting food and water and recognizing friend or foe The vomeronasal (Jacobson's) organ in the roof of the mouth 'tastes' certain smells to help the dog analyse and react to them faster.

THE EARS

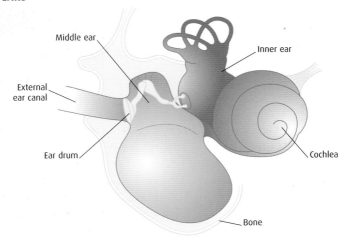

Middle ear

Inner ear

External ear canal

Ear drum

Cochlea

Bone

THE EYES

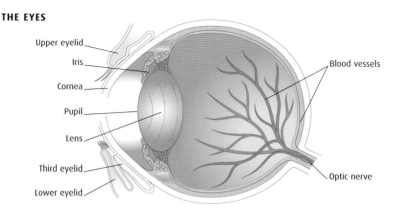

Upper eyelid
Iris
Cornea
Pupil
Lens
Third eyelid
Lower eyelid

Blood vessels
Optic nerve

Taste – canine taste is not thought to be as well developed as a human's in detecting sweet, sour, salty and bitter tastes (dogs have approximately 1,700 taste buds compared to our 10,000). However, dogs are known to have a sweet tooth so anything sweet-smelling or tasting, such as chocolate and antifreeze, should be kept out of their reach as both may prove fatal if ingested.

Sight – canine vision is inferior to humans during the day but is superior at night. Their peripheral vision is better than ours, and research has shown that they can see in colour but only to a limited extent. They have difficulty distinguishing the light colour spectrum between green, red and orange, but can distinguish black, blue, yellow and shades of

DOGS' COLOUR VISION

The human's view

The dog's view

grey. Green(ish) colours are seen as 'white' and red(ish) colours as varying shades of yellow.

Touch – dogs use their noses, mouths and paws to examine objects, after first checking them out by smell. Some dogs are more sensitive to touch than others, depending on life experience and skin/coat thickness. Extra-sensitive areas include the head, feet, mouth, tails and genitals.

Communication

Dogs evolved as pack animals that had to compete with others for food and mates, and these traits are still there beneath the surface of domesticity. Main canine character traits are dependence, sociability, affection, opportunism, instinctiveness, cunning, being predatory, competitiveness, stealth, possessiveness, assertiveness, playfulness and hierarchal.

Vocabulary – dogs have a limited ability to communicate using sound, which comprises whines, squeaks, barking, howling and growling, so they reply more on body language (see pages 38–39). The range of sounds they use tends to be used to back up their body language rather than in isolation.

Dog 'speak' – howling and growling are the least common sounds dogs make, but barking is used frequently to convey a variety of

Key fact
Licking faces has its origins in the behaviour of puppies who lick the mouths of adult dogs in an attempt to get them to regurgitate, or drop, food for them to eat.

meanings – from guarding barks to those designed to get attention, let off steam when excited or when feeling frustrated. By howling, dogs communicate with others who are far away as a way of summoning or finding them.

Mental state – this can be gauged by a dog's posture, facial and body expressions. Generally a stiff stance with jerky movement indicates aggression, uncertainty or fear, while a relaxed body and smooth movement denotes a dog at ease.

Information gathering – dogs gather much information about their world and others species, via scents, particularly from the urine and faeces left by other dogs, and (embarrassingly for us) human crotches. On meeting, dogs sniff each other to find out their sex and intentions.

Aggression – dogs only attack if they deem it necessary for their own safety and well-being, either because something they value is being threatened, or they have learned that attack is the best form of defence. Some breeds, such as terriers, are more inclined to chase and, if they get hold of them, kill, smaller animals, due to their strong chase drive.

Key question
Why does my dog howl at night?
This could be in response to your pet hearing other dogs howling, so is reciprocating to communicate with them. In aged dogs, night-time noise could be a sign of canine senile dementia (see pages 174–175) or geriatric separation anxiety (see pages 144–145) or it could be due to separation anxiety. Alternatively, if the dog is unneutered, he or she is calling for a mate or senses a potential mate nearby. It is also possible that your dog is in pain, so a veterinary check-up would be wise as the first course of action.

Tail-wagging – this is a quick and easy way of communicating his mood, although it is not always a sign of a friendly and happy dog. Different tail positions and the speed of wagging combined with other body language can all convey information. See pages 38–39 for more on reading your dog's body language, combining signs from the dog's stance, ears, pawing and hackles.

Body language

Dogs have a language unique to them, but if we observe them carefully we can get a detailed picture of their body language and actions that helps us guess how they are feeling, what they want from us and what they need. Dogs observe us, too, in order to learn the most advantageous way for them to behave around us.

Baring the teeth agressively – this is a dog's way of telling something to 'back off' and leave him alone. An 'adversary's' retreat should be slow and obvious to avoid being attacked. Sudden moves could provoke an assault in this highly tense situation.

Relaxed smile – this happy pose signifies a playful dog, who is inviting others to interact with him. Many dogs do this as a greeting and 'smile' to show their passive and playful intentions.

Cowering – a wary dog will try to shrink away from something he is uncertain about: this is a posture that often indicates he's had an unpleasant experience in the past of whatever it is that approaches him, whether that be human or another species type.

Yawning – constant yawning and licking lips indicates that a dog is uneasy about a situation he is in.

QUICK GUIDE TO YOUR DOG'S BODY LANGUAGE

Ears   Lolling (flopping) means the dog is relaxed; pricked means the dog is attentive; cocked to one side with ears raised means the dog is listening intently to pinpoint and identify a sound; flat back usually signals depression, fear, nervousness or tension/aggression, depending on the rest of the body stance

Body stance   See 'Mental state' on page 37. Shrinking back with tail between legs indicates wariness or fear; play-bowing (legs stretched out in front with the front end low to the floor) is a playful stance

Tail   Energetic wagging at half-mast is usually a good sign when it comes complete with a relaxed body stance, 'smiley' face and lolling ears; wagging a stiff, raised tail implies tension and potential aggression – especially if combined with raised hackles stiff-leggedness and a fixed-eye expression; while wagging a low tail, possibly between his legs, indicates a fearful and/or submissive dog

Pawing   Often a method to get attention, if the head is up and he's focused on something. Pawing with head lowered signifies submissiveness

Hackles   This is the area at the top of the shoulders, just behind the neck. When raised, the hair stands on end and bushes out – often extending along the spine – and indicates the dog is on his guard and ready to attack if he deems it necessary

Sniffing – an investigative dog determinedly sniffs an object he wants to learn more about, or if he scents something on them that could prove to his advantage, such as food in a pocket.

Rolling – a dog lying on his back, exposing his belly and leaving himself vulnerable denotes submission. Depending on the situation, it's often a good way to get himself out of receiving punishment.

Reproduction

In entire and mature canines, the urge to procreate is strong to ensure survival of the species. A healthy bitch with access to male dogs and a plentiful food supply can produce two litters a year. Generally, big dogs have large litters – with 20 or more puppies being recorded in breeds, such as Great Danes and Neapolitan Mastiffs.

Oestrus – this term denotes when a bitch is ready to breed; it's also known as 'in season' or 'in heat'. It happens approximately every six months and lasts approximately 21 days. It is signified by a bloody vaginal discharge at the beginning of the oestrus.

Key question
Can dogs mate at any time?
Male dogs can, but bitches only come into oestrus twice a year and it is only then that they are receptive to sexual advances from canine suitors.

Mating – this only occurs 10–14 days into the oestrus, when the discharge runs clear. During mating, the dog and bitch may become 'tied', whereby the bitch's vaginal muscles contract around the penis so the dog cannot escape, thus enhancing the chance of conception. This can last for up to 30 minutes and the pair should not be forcibly separated otherwise pain will, and injury may, occur.

Pregnancy – canine gestation lasts for approximately 63 days (nine weeks). As

giving birth approaches, bitches will often start to 'nest', that is, seeking a private, safe and usually dark place in which to give birth.

Birth – as the birthing process begins, she will pace around restlessly, appear anxious, pant and whine, and look behind her in an agitated and puzzled manner. This stage can last up to 24 hours. In second stage labour, the bitch goes to her nesting place, lies on her side and strains as uterine contractions move the puppies, one at a time, down the birth canal. Once uterine contractions start, the puppies quickly follow at 10–60 minute intervals. If the bitch appears distressed, or no puppies appear,

seek veterinary attention immediately in case a puppy is stuck. Most bitches give birth easily without problems or human interference, and instinctively know how to care for their puppies.

Size of litter – the number of puppies in a litter is normally naturally regulated by the size of the bitch. Small bitches usually have up to six puppies, medium bitches up to eight and large up to 12 or more. Generally she has no more than the number of functional nipples she has. In abnormally large litters, some puppies have to be hand-fed or fostered.

Puppy care

How puppies are brought up, handled
and socialized with people and other
animals has a great bearing on the
adult dogs they'll become. Do it right,
and you'll have a happy, healthy,
affectionate and well-mannered four-
legged best friend for life – a dog you
will be proud of and one that everyone
will want to own. Dogs deserve no less.

Where to get a puppy

From the amateur breeder to the professional, puppy mills to animal shelters, there are many options for finding a puppy. Local papers often have many advertisements listing puppies of all sorts of breeds and types, and vets' noticeboards, family and friends are other potential sources. All, however, have their pros and cons, therefore it pays to take your time and shop around.

Tips for making the right choice

Before you succumb to the cute eyes and wagging tail, it often pays to do your homework and ask the right questions to ensure that your puppy is healthy and comes from a well-cared for home. It is worth finding a reputable breeder who screens their breeding stock for hereditary ailments.

- Can you meet the dog's parents and assess their temperament?
- Is the puppy alert and sociable?
- For pedigree breeds, check for hereditary ailments.
- Has the puppy had its required vaccinations?

FINDING A PUPPY

Source	Where to find	Pros	Cons	Price
Amateur breeder	Local papers and via word of mouth	Puppies are often well socialized as part of the family	Hereditary disease health checks are not always carried out	Usually cheaper than pro breeders
Professional (pro) breeder	Usually experienced in producing good examples of a breed	Stock usually screened for hereditary diseases	Problems in some lines may not become apparent until years later	Premium
Puppy mill	Local papers, telephone directories and via Internet	View many breeds under one roof	Stock is often unhealthy and unsocialized	Premium
Animal shelter	Newspapers and Internet	Homing an unwanted puppy	The puppy's history is often unknown	Usually a fee to adopt
Vets' noticeboard	Veterinary clinics	Puppies are often free	Given as seen	Often no cost
Newspapers & dog magazines	Newsagents	Lots of choice	Breeder or puppy history may not be known	Varies
Family & friends	Word of mouth	History of puppy is often known	You may have to wait for a puppy to be available	Free to expensive
Stray	Wandering with no identification collar tag	Rescuing an unwanted puppy	You usually need to report it to the authorities and see if it is claimed. It may be ID microchipped	Free

Puppy kit

Getting a puppy is an exciting time – there is so much to look forward to, not least shopping for canine equipment. There's a huge range available, but you simply need the basics to make life more comfortable for both you and your new friend.

Collar – choose one in leather, natural fabric or synthetic material of the appropriate weight and width. There should be enough room to insert two fingers under it, and check it regularly as puppies grow fast. Wash, or change, the collar often.

Lead – ensure it is comfortable for you to hold, and of a suitable length to maintain slack tension. A retractable nylon leash gives you the best of both worlds.

Key item
Collar identity disc – this should display your name and current phone number(s), both mobile and landline. You can also have your puppy microchipped or tattooed to aid identification if he becomes lost (see page 87).

Food and water bowls – buy bowls that are easily cleaned and are non-chewable. Ceramic or stainless steel bowls are ideal. Plastic ones tend to harbour smells after a while so should be changed regularly.

Bed and bedding – a puppy will be happy with a thick cardboard box. When buying a solid bed, get one that will be big enough for the puppy when he reaches adulthood. A tough plastic dog bed is easily washed and

dried. Bedding should be thick and warm and washed weekly for hygiene's sake.

Crate – a dog crate is useful as a bed, for toilet-training and for when travelling.

Poop scoop – use plastic carrier, food bags or biodegradable nappy bags. Dispose of faeces in public waste bins, designated dog waste bins or in your household rubbish.

Grooming kit – you'll need a brush suitable for your pet's coat type, dog shampoo and a canine toothbrush and toothpaste to help maintain oral health.

Toys – give your puppy toys to play with, to give him something to chew (especially when teething) and help with training.

Puppy toys

Avoid small balls that could get stuck in the throat or flimsy plastic or fabric toys that could be easily shredded and swallowed. Suitable playthings and teething aids include:

- 'Indestructible' toys, such as conical rubber chews filled with treats or food (with air holes at each end to avoid suction injuries) or flavoured rubber chew bones for puppies
- Puppy teething keys or rubber rings

- Strong rubber tug toys
- Puppy dental chews
- Tough rope raggers

Feeding puppies

The best way to help your puppy grow into a healthy and sound adult is to feed a suitable diet, keeping it simple and choosing the best quality food you can afford. Breeders usually provide a diet sheet stating what to feed their puppies, how much and when. Make any changes to diet brands gradually to avoid upset stomachs.

Easy feeding – look for 'famous name' puppy food brands, as these comprise a balanced diet for growing puppies. Some manufacturers also produce a specific 'breed feed', both for puppies and adults, formulated to a particular type's life stage

Key fact
Puppies need more calories per day than adults in relation to their body weight because they are growing rapidly, are more subject to heat loss due to their small size and their energy requirements are higher.

and bodily needs. Choose foods with as few artificial ingredients as possible. See pages 90–93 for food types and amounts to feed.

Amount to feed – be guided by the guidelines given on the food packs, although these often err on the generous side, which can lead to your puppy gaining too much weight for his growing bones, joints and ligaments to bear easily, thus putting undue strain on them. Split the recommended total

daily ration into 2–4 smaller feeds (see 'Puppy Feeding Guide', right) so as not to overload the stomach.

What to feed – there's usually no need to add anything else to specially formulated complete puppy foods. If dry food, ensure it is thoroughly soaked before feeding to avoid it expanding in the stomach and causing bloat or blockages. Add puppy mixer meal or biscuits to tinned or foil/plastic-packaged puppy meat.

Water – always ensure your puppy has a supply of fresh, clean water, ideally situated near his feeding bowl or his crate or bed.

PUPPY FEEDING GUIDE

Age	Number of meals per day
Weaning–20 weeks	3–4, plus a dish of puppy formula milk
20–30 weeks	3
30 weeks–9 months	2
Over 9 months	1–2

New arrival

Bringing a new puppy home can be overwhelming for a young dog, so how you collect him and treat him in the first 24 hours in your house is crucial to ensuring that he perceives you and his strange, new surroundings in a good light. Aim to make your puppy's first hours and days with you as calm as possible.

Timing – if you work, arrange to pick up your puppy when you have a couple of days off to help him settle in. Avoid bringing a new puppy into your life if you are in the throes of moving house, are expecting a baby, are ill or if things are tense for some reason.

Car travel – transport the puppy in a travel crate for everyone's safety. Drive carefully, braking and taking corners gradually and smoothly. Ensure there is enough cool air flow in the car and avoid travelling in the heat of the day.

On arrival – take him to the garden or yard first to let him toilet if needed, praising him if he 'performs', then show him his quiet 'den' area (the crate can double as this) inside, which is where he should be able to rest and escape to in peace. Let him investigate, without over-fussing him. Ensure he has fresh water available and put food

treats and toys in your puppy's den to confirm that it's a good place to be.

First steps – giving your puppy an activity toy to play with will help keep him occupied and happy, taking his mind off the unfamiliar

sounds, smells and surroundings. Try to stick to his usual feed times, and take him outside to toilet afterwards – he'll soon become toilet-trained.

Quiet time – puppies sleep a lot, so it's essential to let him do so undisturbed when he wants and not to overexcite him or tire him out with lots of fuss and visitors in his first few days.

Bedtime – he may whine for the first couple of nights because he's missing his mother and siblings, but he'll gradually get used to being on his own. It may help settle a distressed puppy to have him in your bedroom – in a puppy pen or travel crate – for the first few nights, gradually moving him further away. Be prepared to have to get up in the night to let him out to toilet while you follow this procedure.

New puppy behaviour

Once he's settled in, your puppy is likely to do things you may find amusing, baffling and irritating in turn. Knowing how he's likely to behave and how to deal with it will make life easier for you both.

all footwear are toys to gnaw on and carry around. Instead, give him rubber teething toys or rawhide chews to help him cut his teeth.

Upset tummy – a change in water and situation can affect digestion, just as it does in humans, so don't worry too much if your puppy's motions are a bit loose for the first day or two. If he looks ill, however, seek veterinary attention immediately. Keep him on the diet his breeder was feeding, and make any changes gradually.

Attention-seeking – a puppy will come to you, as his provider of comfort and food, for reassurance, affection and to play with in the absence of his mother and littermates. Give attention in moderation only, reserving special attention for when he displays desirable behaviours. A puppy must be gradually taught to become more independent, otherwise he'll be demanding your attention all the time.

Chewing – puppies use their mouths to investigate things, and help them bring through their adult teeth. This can, unwittingly, lead them into trouble. Tape wires out of his way, and don't leave things lying around that you don't want chewing. Don't give him old slippers and shoes to play with, as he'll think

Play-biting – discourage this by substituting a toy for your hand if play becomes rough. Puppy teeth are sharp, and encouraging him to grab at you when he's small may be funny now – but it could turn into dangerous behaviour when he's older.

Toys – as with food, puppies should not be allowed to become possessive over toys. See page 54 for how to deal with this type of behaviour.

Toileting inside
Until he's been taught otherwise (see page 60), your puppy will do what comes naturally, wherever and whenever – so expect accidents and don't punish him for them.

Getting to know you

How you handle your puppy has bearing on how he views you and your family, as being trustworthy humans to be with. A puppy relies on his owners to take good care of him, and will learn from how he is handled, so it's important that you get it right initially in order to cement a great relationship.

Young love – it's important to teach children how to pick up and handle puppies (see opposite). Always ensure that they interact under adult supervision for safety's sake.

Naming – choose a name for your puppy that's easy to say – one or two syllables is best as it rolls off the tongue, such as 'Bus-ter',

'Prince', 'Dee-for' (dog!) and so forth. Always say it in a positive, happy and encouraging way, opening your arms in a welcoming gesture as you do so, and within days your puppy will learn that this sound is his cue to come to you for attention.

Strangers – show people how to handle him; crouching down to greet him and letting him come to them to sniff and reassure himself. Strangers towering above him can be terrifying for a young puppy. Request they keep their voices calm so as not to scare him and teach them how to address him and how to prevent him getting over-excited and jumping up or play-biting (see pages 56–57 and 124–125).

Happy meals

In the litter, puppies learn to be possessive of their food. This may result in them growling or snapping at humans who go near them while eating, so discourage this behaviour by giving him half his meal and adding the rest while he's eating. This teaches him that hands and people near his bowl are rewarding, not threatening.

HOW TO PICK UP AND CARRY YOUR PUPPY

1 Crouch down and call your puppy (see 'Naming', left). Gently, but firmly, gather him to you, with one arm around his chest to keep him from breaking free, and the other arm under his bottom for support.

2 Keep him close to you so that he feels safe and cannot jump from your arms, and stand up slowly.

3 Carry him close to your chest, vocally reassuring him. To put him down, simply reverse the action.

Playing with your puppy

Puppies have seemingly boundless energy and, as they are so cute, it's very tempting to play for hours with them. Just like human babies, though, they tire quickly and can become fretful so be certain he gets enough rest and undisturbed time to relax. Remember, playing with your puppy needs to be on your terms, not his.

Be patient – naturally you'll want to spend lots of time playing with your puppy, and taking him for walks, but don't over-do it. Growing bones and developing ligaments, muscles and tendons can get damaged if too much stress is put on them. Being patient will really pay off in the long run when you'll be the proud owner of a physically and mentally healthy mature dog.

Playtime repertoire – ideal interactive and bonding games to play, either inside or outside – that also teach basic manners – include hide-and-seek (hide strong-smelling treats or toys in easy to find places for your puppy to find); playing 'tug', teaching your puppy to let go when you want him to; and rolling a ball or throwing a softer toy for him to chase and encouraging him to bring it back to you. Avoid strenuous activity to prevent injury.

Play dates – it's good, once he's fully vaccinated, to allow your puppy to meet and play with others of his kind, of the same age and older. Puppy classes are ideal for this, so that initial introductions are done in a safe and controlled manner (see pages 74–75).

Ankle-biters

Children, especially, have great fun with puppies and naturally want to happily run around when playing with them, but the trouble is that an over-excited puppy may end up following his natural instincts and chasing with the intent of 'catching and eating' his 'prey'. So avoid having to patch up your kids' nipped ankles by teaching them not to play 'chase' with puppy until he's older, and trained, enough to know better.

A little respect – puppies may need to learn the hard way that established pets, especially cats, may not take kindly to an exuberant puppy bounding up to them hoping for a game. After a couple of swipes from a cat's paw, he will soon learn his place.

DEMANDING ATTENTION

1 Don't let your puppy demand attention any time he wants it, or he'll become a nuisance, both to you and with visitors. If he does try to get your attention when you don't want him to, perhaps by jumping up or pawing at you, gently push him away.

2 Look away from him and ignore him until he stops bothering you and remains quiet.

3 Now you can reward him for being quiet, patient and undemanding. Through the use of food motivation and reward, your puppy will learn that he gets attention when you want to give it and not when he demands it.

Growing up

Your puppy will grow up rapidly and knowing what to expect from him – and when to expect it – as he's maturing will help you understand more about him and aid the bonding process between you. Building a great, mutual relationship takes patience and time – but you can look forward to each day being full of fun.

Toilet-training

Puppies need to be taught not to relieve themselves in the house, but expect a few accidents at first. Whether outside in the garden, or inside in a designated area, toilet-training is simple to teach and a puppy will soon learn if you are patient and give him lots of praise for appropriate toileting.

Toilet trips – puppies need to relieve themselves frequently, so be prepared to take him outside a lot – especially after he's woken up or eaten as that's when he's most likely to want to go.

Praise him – give praise immediately for toileting outside, or wherever his toilet area is (you can get indoor toilet trays for dogs if required), then he soon learns that his actions are rewarding.

Clear signal – leave your puppy's last droppings in place then he knows where to go next time by sight and smell. Once he's learned where to go, clear up and dispose of droppings (see page 47) as soon as he's done them.

Key question
Is it correct to rub a puppy's nose in his mess to stop him doing it inside again?
No, never do this. It does not work and will only scare your puppy.

Recognize the signs – if your puppy is going to relieve himself he may pace the floor, whine, refuse to settle, look anxious, go to the door or sneak off behind furniture, so be quick to spot this behaviour and take him to his toilet area. Do this gently and calmly and praise him when he 'performs'.

Accidents – until he's fully toilet-trained, put newspapers down in the area your puppy occupies so that any mess is easier to clean up. Do not shout at, or smack, a puppy for toileting in the house as he's only doing what comes naturally – he won't understand why you are reprimanding him and will become frightened of you.

Neutering

Whether or not you choose to have your young dog neutered is up to you, but this procedure can help prevent various problems occurring as he or she matures. Male dogs are castrated, while females (bitches) are spayed. It's a myth that dogs will suffer from not reproducing – what they don't know they won't miss.

Neutering surgery – this is performed under anaesthetic. Males have their testicles removed, while bitches have their ovaries, Fallopian tubes and uterus taken out. Wounds are then closed using stitches. Dogs will usually go home the same day and any discomfort can be controlled with medication.

BENEFITS OF NEUTERING	
Males	**Females**
Removes the sexual urge and inclination to wander off	Prevents unwanted pregnancies
Helps prevent sexual frustration and leg mounting	Stops problems and mess associated with oestrus
Certain types of potential aggression are reduced	Removes the urge to wander off in search of a mate
The risk of hormone-related diseases and testicular cancers are lessened	No more unwanted attention from entire male dogs
Reduces the risk of prostate gland problems and sexually transmitted diseases	Decreased risk of uterine infections and mammary, uterine and ovarian cancers
Dogs are usually calmer and more reliable	Bitches are usually calmer and more reliable

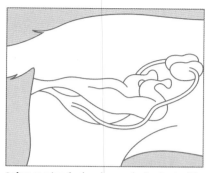

Before spaying the female reproductive tract: with ovaries, Fallopian tubes and womb (uterus).

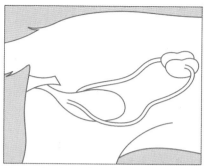

After spaying the ovaries, Fallopian tubes and womb have been removed.

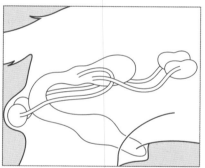

Before castration two testicles are connected to the penis via the spermatic cords (vas deferens).

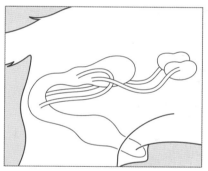

After castration the testicles and part of the spermatic cords have been removed.

Key question

Is it best to let a bitch have a litter before she is spayed?

There is no evidence to suggest this is necessary, and allowing her to do so will add to the population of unwanted dogs unless you can be certain you can find good, permanent homes for the puppies.

Mouth matters

A dog's mouth is extremely important to him since he uses it to eat, drink, investigate and communicate so you need to help him maintain it in tiptop order so that it functions efficiently and without discomfort to him.

Two sets of teeth – puppies shed their non-permanent (milk) teeth between 3 and 6 months as their adult (permanent) set grows and pushes through the gums (see pages 30–31). The first permanent teeth to crown are the two centre teeth (incisors) on the top jaw and the last are the large corner (canine) teeth in both bottom and top jaws.

Teething – while he's teething your puppy may become fretful and he'll want to chew anything he can get his jaws around in an effort to ease oral discomfort and itching. Give him toys and rawhide chews to gnaw on and then he'll be less likely to chew household objects and furniture.

Problems – these can occur if milk teeth are not shed before the permanent teeth come through, particularly in Toy breeds. This can cause discomfort as well as distorting the shape of the mouth and eating and digestion problems can result. In such cases veterinary attention should be sought.

Smelly breath – if you feed your puppy a diet of meat and crunchy mixer biscuits it will help stimulate gum circulation and remove accumulated plaque, thereby reducing the likelihood of bad breath.

Key question
I've seen dental chews and special oral hygiene dog food in the pet shop. Should I give these to my puppy?
Dental chews help a puppy cut his adult teeth and keep them clean, but only give them under supervision. Choose only chews and periodontal food formulated for puppies, as adult varieties will be unsuitable.

Complete foods that are fed moistened tend to cling to teeth, and accumulated plaque hardens into tartar. Clean your dog's teeth weekly to keep plaque at bay (see pages 80–81). Toys designed for chewing help to promote saliva flow, and help keep plaque at bay thereby aiding oral health.

Sexual maturity

At around 5–6 months of age, dogs reach puberty and are attracted to sexually active members of their kind in order to mate and reproduce. Smaller breeds develop more quickly than large ones. At this age, hormonal changes start taking place in your puppy's body, ready for them to become parents themselves.

Bitches – females reach puberty at 6–7 months, but this can happen at 4 months, while others may not have their first season (see pages 40–41) until 1–2 years of age. Bitches should be at least 12–18 months old, depending on the breed, before they are bred from in order to allow them time to mature.

Dogs – males are normally indifferent to bitches that are not in season, but will be attracted to her when her body releases the chemicals known as pheromones indicating her sexual condition. This happens a few days before she becomes sexually receptive, which explains why males are so excited by bitches who are not ready to receive their advances and who repulse them fiercely.

Unwanted attention – canine suitors may gather outside your house when your bitch comes into season; she will do her utmost to escape and be mated, while they will try hard to get to her. Some sexually active dogs are so determined to find a mate that they will go to any lengths to escape and do so. Fending off determined suitors when walking a bitch in season is risky – you may get bitten or dog fights may occur, so it's safer not to take her out in this condition, but exercise in the garden only. Or, if you know of areas you can

walk her where it's unlikely you'll meet other dogs, take her there but keep her on a lead to prevent her running off in search of a mate.

Mood swings – as they reach sexual maturity, young dogs may display undesirable, but natural, behaviours such as urine scent marking or soiling in the house to mark their territory and availability, overly seeking attention, mounting human legs and soft toys, and sometimes showing aggression. There is not much you can do to prevent or cure this, other than have your pet neutered, since such behaviour may remain into adulthood. Sometimes, engaging in regular exercise and activities, such as agility, can help channel energy into more positive behaviour, so that is worth a try. Young entire canines often practise mating behaviour with other dogs of both sexes.

Life stages

Your puppy will grow and mature at a rapid rate. The examples below show you what to expect at the different stages in his development, from dependence on their mother to when best to introduce solid food and start training.

Newborn puppies These are totally dependent on their mother and her milk for the first three weeks. Eyes are sealed shut for the first 10 days or so.

2–3 weeks Begin to handle the puppies from two weeks to begin the vital canine-human socialization process. Their milk teeth appear and they learn to walk and lap liquid food. Their senses of sight, smell and hearing begin to operate.

4–5 weeks Puppies can now see more clearly, stand and toddle around. They begin to play, start to bark and wag their tails. They will be eating a more solid puppy food, leaving the sleeping area to toilet and are curious.

6 weeks Puppies now have full use of their eyes and ears. Weaning onto puppy foods proper can be introduced.

7–11 weeks Puppies are now usually fully weaned, socialized with humans and other household pets, and are ready to go to new homes. Toilet- and name-training can begin, as can teaching him manners and obedience.

Juvenile (12 weeks–6 months) Puppies are playful. Chewing and mouthing behaviour is common, especially when they are teething (see pages 64–65). Training needs to be done on a daily basis (see pages 70–71).

Adolescent (6–18 months) Sexual maturity is usually reached (see pages 66–67) and this is often the most difficult time for owners to live through. If you have laid down solid foundations of good behaviour up to now, adolescence will be less wearing for everyone.

Adult (18 months and over) Most dogs will now be physically mature, and their characters fully formed – although some refinements will still be occurring and young adults finally settle down at around 3 years of age. Maintain regular training.

Early learning

In order to grow into an amenable, well mannered, housetrained and obedient adult, a puppy needs to be taught how to be all of these things. Training begins when you bring your puppy home, usually at eight weeks of age – see the initial five-week training plan opposite. Puppies are eager to please but keep training sessions short so as not to overtax their bodies and brains.

FIVE-WEEK TRAINING PLAN

Week 1   Teach him to recognize and answer to his name (see pages 54–55)

Begin socializing: accustom him to household sights and sounds – other pets, television, washing machine, vacuum cleaner, etc. (see pages 76–77)

Handle puppy while he is eating (see pages 54–55)

Toilet-train (see pages 60–61)

Week 2   Commence collar and leash training (see pages 104–105)

Let puppy meet people of all ages, sexes and appearances

Begin any behavioural training as necessary, such as for play-biting (see pages 52–53)

Week 3   Sight-introduce puppy to animals such as cattle, horses and sheep. Do not allow him to chase them – keep him in your arms or on a lead

Week 4   Introduce car travel, ensuring he's properly secured in a travel crate. Avoid doing so after feeding, otherwise he may vomit

After being fully vaccinated, begin taking him for short walks close to home, day and night, to accustom him to sights and sounds. Also start going to puppy classes (see pages 74–75)

Week 5   Gradually extend car journeys – but never on warm days as cars soon get too hot for dogs

Begin basic training for obedience and manners (see pages 100–125) in short five-minute spells, as puppies have a limited attention span and tire quickly. End sessions on a positive note, even if it means going back a step

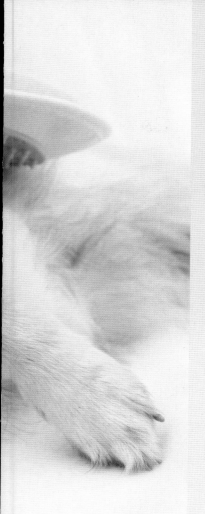

Routine care

In order to stay safe, happy and healthy in mind and body, puppies need their owners to carry out various actions for them on a regular basis. These include training and socialization, grooming, dental care and health checks. Interacting with your dog is a great way of bonding with him and you'll get a good deal of satisfaction from knowing, and seeing, that he is physically and mentally fit and well.

Puppy school

Puppy socialization classes are the equivalent of a human nursery school. It's here that your puppy will be able to carry on mixing with other puppies, as he would with his siblings in the litter, and learning how to meet, greet and play with them in a controlled environment.

People skills – your puppy will also get the chance to meet lots of other people at puppy classes, and learn how to interact with them, and this is another vital element of his social upbringing.

Respect for their elders – contact with adult dogs is needed, too. Some trainers take along their own dogs to teach puppies respect for their elders but who will not become aggressive.

Where and when – weekly classes are often held at veterinary clinics, run by vet nurses, and many dog trainers hold 'nursery' classes, too. Ask puppy-owning friends if they can recommend somewhere they've been to. Avoid places that have slippery floors to prevent accidents.

How often? – take your puppy as many times as you are able, the more the better, and ensure that you attend regularly. Aim to go at least once a week, preferably more, until your puppy is judged ready by you and the trainer to begin training classes, and then aim to go to these at least once a week on a permanent basis to maintain obedience and sociability, and help keep bad habits from developing in both you and your pet.

What should I look for? – check that all youngsters are of a similar size, age and temperament, to avoid scaring small or timid puppies. Ensure the class is properly supervised, and that all introductions are done on lead.

Hierarchy – puppies soon find an acceptable level of play and chase and sort out the pecking order among themselves. However, ensure it doesn't become a rambunctious free-for-all with behaviour that becomes too rough or bullying.

Key question
How do I lead-train a puppy?

Simply pop the collar on your puppy for short spells initially, praise, reward and play with him to distract him and he'll soon get used to it. Attach a lead but don't drag him on it – just crouch down, gently draw on it, call puppy to you and reward him for doing so. He'll soon catch on. (See pages 104–105 for more on lead training.)

Socialization

Puppies are naturally sociable and curious during the critical socialization period between four and 18 weeks, so during this time gradually introduce him to as many different everyday situations, sights, smells and sounds as possible to get him used to the world he lives in.

Noise abatement – sounds such as music, the telephone, television and washing machine can panic a puppy (remember his hearing is much keener than ours and he will find loud noise uncomfortable), so turn the volume down when possible until he gets used to them.

Vacuuming – put puppy in another room close by with an activity toy or tasty chew when you first vacuum so he gets used to the scary noise, then use a door-gate so he can see it, realize it won't hurt him and know it is nothing to worry about.

People – introduce puppy to as many people of all ages and appearances as possible, to teach him that humans are rewarding to be with. See pages 54–55 on how to approach new people and social situations. Ensure puppy interacts with males and females equally so he's at ease with both sexes.

Gotcha! – get puppy used to being grabbed suddenly, as there'll be times when someone will do this to him, especially when he meets young children or if someone needs to grab him quickly for safety's sake. Reward him when you do it so he learns that it's not threatening.

Getting to know the vet

Choose a vet that specializes in canines, and one that you feel at ease with and can talk to. Local trainers can usually recommend a good one. If possible, take your puppy along to visit the clinic regularly for a fuss and treat from the vet nurse (many clinics encourage this), so that he doesn't just associate the practice with unpleasant treatments, and thus reduces his (and your stress) on visits.

Road sense – if possible, carry puppy for the first couple of times when you introduce him to traffic as the size and sound of vehicles may alarm him (see pages 108–109). Dogs should be on a lead and under control at all times near roads, no matter how well you think he is trained.

Other pets – make introductions to other dogs or cats in the house under supervision and remove food bowls and toys that could cause possessive aggression. It's best to let a new puppy meet an existing dog on unfamiliar ground, so he doesn't resent an

'intruder' on his territory. Once acquainted, take them home and allow them to interact in a calm atmosphere but maintain a close watch to ensure peace reigns. Don't fuss the puppy more than the existing dog – ensure both receive enough attention to prevent jealous aggression from the older pet.

Out and about – going for a walk is a great way for your puppy to meet and greet people and other dogs. Take care that introductions with other dogs are done on-lead and, initially, avoid interaction with overly boisterous dogs so that your puppy is not frightened.

Simple health checks

Keeping a close eye on your puppy on a daily basis enables you to learn what his usual weight, toileting habits, demeanour, behaviour and character comprises. Any change from the norm should be noted in case it heralds a potential problem that needs to be addressed.

Vital signs – (see pages 158–159). Taking and noting your puppy's temperature, pulse and respiration rates (TPR) regularly, on warm and cool days, at rest and after exercise, will enable you to gauge his average TPR, then you'll know that any significant change in these may be a cause for concern, especially together with other physical or mental changes.

Demeanour – depression, restlessness, ear-shaking or scratching, hunching up, lack of

energy or appetite, stiffness or limping needs veterinary attention, as does over-reacting to sound, light and touch or a swollen abdomen.

Coat – the coat should be shiny in most breeds and free from ticks and fleas. Excessive hair loss should be investigated by a vet to ascertain the cause and suggest a solution. Ask your canine beautician to show you how to keep puppy's nails at the right length. Run your hands over puppy daily to check for unusual lumps, bumps, heat or swelling that may need veterinary attention.

Oral hygiene – look at puppy's mouth and teeth daily to get him used to this procedure and check for problems. Gnawing on large, raw, meaty bones helps keep teeth free from plaque and gums healthy.

Eyes – wipe your puppy's eyes with tepid water and cotton wool to remove discharge. Normal discharge comprises occasional dark-coloured accumulated matter, whereas the appearance of yellow or green discharge indicates something is wrong and it should be investigated by a vet.

Toileting – faeces should be firm, not sloppy, nor contain worms, while urine should be clear yellow. Blood should not be present in either. There should be no excessive straining on urination or defecation. Eliminations are a useful indicator of canine health.

Weight – your vet will tell you what your puppy's ideal weight should be, and as he reaches adulthood. Aim to maintain the ideal (see pages 92–93 for a guide to weights and feeding). Obesity causes all sorts of problems, including joint and heart ailments.

Key question
My puppy seems to urinate a lot. Is this normal?
Puppies do tend to urinate a lot, but this lessens as they grow older and are able to contain their bladder more effectively. If, however, he appears to be in pain (such as straining or crying) when urinating, seek veterinary advice immediately.

Grooming

Not only does grooming your dog on a daily or weekly basis, depending on his type of coat, help keep his skin and coat in good condition, it's also a fantastic way of bonding with him and an excellent way of getting him used to being handled all over. This is also a great way to involve older children in the care and responsibility of their pet.

How to groom – this depends on your puppy's coat type. If the coat is anything but a short, smooth one, ask the breeder for grooming advice and what brushes to use in the first instance. Generally, though, a short-bristled brush is fine. Longhaired coats are usually easily groomed out with a slicker brush and a wide-toothed comb. Some breeds, such as Poodles and corded-coat types, need professional grooming and clipping every six weeks or so.

Grooming checklist

- Shears or scissors (use with care)
- Suitable brushes and combs
- Cottonwool for eyes, ears and genitals
- Canine toothbrush and toothpaste

Skin care – put puppy on a table with a non-slip mat to make grooming easier and put less strain on your back. Hold him securely so he cannot jump off. Be careful not to drag the coat or pull on the skin as this will cause your puppy discomfort. Puppy will soon say if you are being too rough. If the coat is very tangled, take him for expert attention.

Important little places – get your puppy used to having his ears, eyes, mouth and genital areas handled so that grooming and vet visits are easier. Wipe under the tail to keep the rear end clean. See pages 78–79 for advice on cleaning ears and eyes.

Clipping and trimming – before attempting to clip or trim a coat, or trim nails, ask an expert groomer to show you how so as to not to make a mess of the coat, or cause nail discomfort and bleeding.

CLEANING TEETH

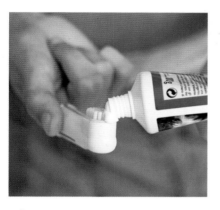

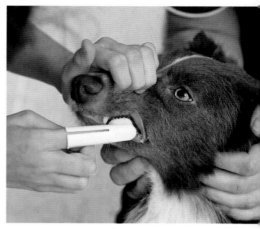

1 Squeeze a little canine (usually meat-flavoured) toothpaste onto a toothbrush or finger brush designed for dogs.

2 Pull back the lips and gently rub toothpaste all over the teeth.

3 A long toothbrush makes brushing back teeth easier.

Key fact

Giving your dog lots of praise while grooming and inspecting him teaches him that this is a pleasant and rewarding procedure to endure patiently.

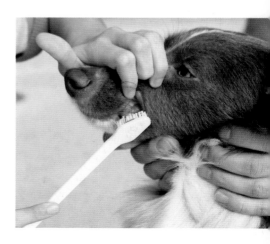

Bath time

Unless your puppy is a small, short-coated breed, it's easier to take him to a groomer who has all the facilities for bathing, drying and grooming afterwards. Dogs usually only need bathing when they get dirty and smelly, such as when they've rolled in something unpleasant or taken a dip in a muddy waterway.

Be careful – never bath a dog with a matted coat as it will make the tangles worse. Groom the tangle out, or clip it off, first. Bathing too often will strip the coat and skin of natural oils and make them dry. Do not use human shampoos and conditioners as the chemicals in these can prove injurious to dogs, either through absorption through the skin or by causing skin and eye irritation.

Bath time checklist
- Bath, sink or large container outside (on a warm day)
- Shower attachment, plastic jug or hose with tepid water
- Rubber mat for secure footing
- Dog shampoo and conditioner
- Towels for drying
- Brush and comb for grooming
- Hairdryer

HOW TO BATH YOUR DOG

1 Groom your dog first with a brush or comb to remove any tangles or matted fur. Soak the dog thoroughly with tepid water, getting right down to the skin.

2 Work in shampoo, massaging your dog all over, but being careful not to get soap or water in his eyes and ears. Rinse thoroughly and apply dog conditioner.

3 Rinse out all traces of conditioner (although you can get leave-in ones), until the water runs clear.

4 Skim off excess water from the coat with your hands, then dry your dog well. If it is a warm day, allow him to dry naturally, otherwise use a hairdryer on a low setting, being careful not to get too close and burn him with hot air.

Massage for dogs

Help prevent your puppy or young dog from stiffening up after exercise by treating him to a relaxing and soothing massage. Not only will this help alleviate the symptoms of lactic acid build-up in muscles, it will help avoid short- and long-term discomfort from muscular stiffness that can lead to joint problems in later life.

Massage – this is a good bonding exercise for dog and owner, but check with your vet first to ensure it is appropriate for your pet. Effleurage is the stroking technique that is applied with one hand with an even pressure from the palm, fingers and fingertips. Use less pressure over joints. Repeat each stroke three times. Aim for 15–20 strokes per minute and massage your dog for about five minutes in all.

Key question
Do I carry out massage on my puppy straight after a walk or exercise?
No, let him relax first. Wait until he's calm, quiet, his breathing is normal and he's had a drink of water if required. Massage can be carried out up to four hours after exercise.

HOW TO MASSAGE

1 Start behind the ears, stroke down in front of the shoulder, finishing on the chest between the front legs.

2 Move to the top of the shoulder and massage down, stopping at the elbow.

3 Next, gently massage down the front of the foreleg to the paw.

4 From the paw, move your hand round to the back of the foot and massage up the back of the leg to the elbow.

5 Place your hand on top of the shoulder with your fingers facing his tail. Massage from the shoulder, down the back either side of the spine, stopping at the groin as shown. Finally, massage down the back and front of the hind legs as before, stopping at the knee. Repeat on the other side of the body.

Safe and secure

Keeping your puppy safe and sound, both at home and out and about, is of paramount importance. Priorities are that he is kept out of harm's way and ensuring that he can be identified and returned to you if he strays.

House safety – keep electrical wires secured, and ensure he cannot get into bins and cupboards and help himself to things that may prove injurious to him. Teach him not to bound out of an open doorway or barge past you on the stairs (see pages 110–111).

Garden safety – keep your garden or yard clear of rubbish, chemicals and tools that could prove dangerous to a curious dog. Avoid putting slug pellets down as dogs often find these palatable and eat them, resulting in illness or even death. Only ever use chemical plant sprays that are animal-

friendly and read the application instructions carefully. Garden or yard fencing needs to be dog-proof to prevent your pet escaping.

Water safety – never let your pet walk on icy ponds lest the ice gives way and he falls in. Avoid letting your dog swim in the sea, rivers or ponds unless you are sure it is safe to do so – deep water, strong currents or debris under the surface can prove fatal to the dog but also to you if try to rescue him.

Out walking – always have your dog on a lead when walking on roads, and around livestock. Keep your eye out for dangerous rubbish. When walking in fields containing livestock, stay close to the perimeter so you can leave quickly if necessary.

ID tags and collars – these are required to be worn by dogs in public places, and should display the owner's name and telephone number(s).

PERMANENT ID – PROS AND CONS

	Pros	Cons
Microchipping	Usually permanent and successful method of ID and dog/owner reunion	Chips can fail
		Dogs may not be scanned, or scanned all over in case of chip migration
		Scanners may fail to pick up a chip if incompatible with the particular brand of chip, or because of low battery/cold weather
		Have caused adverse reactions (eg ill health through malignant tumours and even death)
		Failure on owners' part to report change of address may lead to non-reunion
		There is currently no one universal standard or database for chips and scanners used by all
Tattooing	Permanent method of ID	Some tattoos can fade with time
	Not as invasive as microchipping	Databases need to be kept updated of owners address details
		Can look unsightly on pricked ear breeds
		If a tattoo register goes out of business, the tattoo can be meaningless since the database may no longer operate
		Tattoos can be altered

Microchipping – a microchip implant with a unique identification number is registered to your pet and your details are added to a national database. The microchip is inserted under the skin, usually between the shoulder blades and is similar to having a vaccination. If your dog is found, a scanner is used to read the chip and trace the owner.

Tattooing – this is another way of permanently identifying your puppy (see box below). A number is stamped on the inside of the ear and your details entered onto a database. As with microchipping, some dogs find this more painful than others, depending on skin sensitivity and thickness.

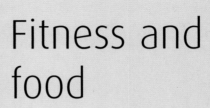

Fitness and food

Feeding a well-balanced diet that is suitable for your breed or type of dog is essential in keeping your pet healthy and happy. There are many brands and types of food to choose from, but taking into account your dog's age, health and lifestyle, and also the vital nutrients he needs, will make this decision easier.

On the menu

There are four forms of commercially prepared dog food comprising wet or moist (canned or pouch), semi-moist (pouch), dry complete and dry complementary (mixer meal or biscuits). You can also buy veterinary diets for dogs with certain diseases, diets without artificial additives and diets formulated for certain breeds.

Commercial foods – these contain all the nutrients dogs need on a daily basis and are quick and easy to feed.

Vegetarian diets – dogs are omnivores and can survive on specially formulated vegetarian diets that contain all the nutrients they need. They do, however, prefer meat. Consult a canine nutrition expert if you are considering a vegeterian diet for your dog.

Natural diets – these comprise either raw or cooked meat mixed with raw or cooked vegetables. This is often referred to as a BARF diet (bones and raw food), but consult your vet first in case it isn't suitable for your dog.

Veterinary diets – these are available at veterinary clinics and should only be fed on veterinary advice. Various types are available for different ailments such as kidney stones, signs of senility, obesity and diabetes mellitus.

Water – dogs need a plentiful supply of clean water available to them at all times. Plan ahead if going on a long walk and take a supply of fresh water with you (see pages 150–151), or if taking your dog on a long car journey.

Hygiene – scrub out water and food bowls daily to keep them clean and sweet-smelling. If suitable, you can wash them in the dishwasher for super cleanliness and sterilization.

Serving – wet food can be fed on its own, but is usually added to complementary food. Dry complementary food is mixed with meat to make up a complete diet, while complete dry food contains everything your dog needs without the need to add anything to it. Semi-moist food is made up of meat mixed with vegetable protein. Feed alone, or mix with complementary biscuits to bulk it out and moisten with water.

Dietary nutrients checklist

- Water
- Protein
- Carbohydrates
- Fat
- Vitamins
- Minerals
- Fibre

Amounts to feed

How much food you give your dog should depend on his age, size, activity level, individual nature and the temperature of his surroundings. Young dogs, and those being worked or are very active on a daily basis, may need more food (calories) per day than the average pet dog, while old, inactive dogs will require less.

Weight-watching – your vet will advise you on the ideal weight for your dog, so aim to maintain this. Weigh him weekly or monthly: either take him to the vet clinic to be weighed (some clinics charge for this), or weigh yourself, then pick up your pet (if possible) and weigh yourself again and subtract the first weight from the second to find out what your dog weighs.

Daily ration – decrease or increase the amount given accordingly depending on his condition and weight. Check how many calories there are in his daily ration – if he's getting enough he'll stay fit and healthy; too many and he'll get fat; not enough will result in him losing condition and becoming underweight.

Calorie-counting – as an example, a small, healthy, adult dog engaging in two hours of average activity daily will require between 125 and 700 calories a day. A large dog will need from 1,400 calories per day to maintain his condition.

APPROXIMATE DAILY FEEDING GUIDE	
Ideal weight of adult dog	Amount of food
2 kg (5 lb)	110–140 g (4–5 oz)
5 kg (10 lb)	200–280 g (7–10 oz)
10 kg (25 lb)	400–570 g (14 oz–1 lb 4 oz)
20 kg (50 lb)	680–900 g (1 lb 8 oz–2 lb)
35 kg (75 lb)	900 g–1.1 kg (2 lb–2 lb 8 oz)
45 kg (100 lb)	1.25–1.6 kg (2 lb 12 oz–3 lb 8 oz)
70 kg (150 lb)	1.7–2.5 kg (3 lb 12 oz–5 lb 8 oz)

Key questions

My dog is extremely active and gets lots of daily exercise. Does he need a high-protein diet to ensure he gets enough energy?

No, a diet higher in fat or carbohydrate is better for very active dogs as these components put less strain on the liver and kidneys than extra protein.

Can I give my dog leftovers as part of his food?

Giving human meal leftovers to your dog is fine, but count them as part of his daily diet to avoid undesirable weight gain. Steer clear of highly spiced food, such as curry, and foodstuffs containing chocolate, alcohol, raisins, grapes, onions and garlic, since these ingredients can prove fatal to some dogs.

Fat or fussy?

Dogs are usually greedy feeders and will eat anything put in front of them, so it's rare to have a fussy eater. On the other hand, some pets are adept at begging for, and getting, more food than they need from their owners, which often leads to them becoming overweight.

Fussy eaters – these are usually created by their owners; a dog won't usually starve himself unless there is a physical reason, such as illness or a mouth problem, so consult your vet in the first instance to rule this out, or treat accordingly.

Curing fussiness – if your dog is healthy, then only give him his regular diet at set times. If it remains uneaten after 20 minutes, remove and dispose of the food. Do not give him anything else until the next set mealtime. This usually works within a day or two.

Fat dogs – this usually occurs by them eating more than is necessary and not having enough daily exercise. Obesity causes all sorts of ailments, from joint problems to heart disease, so it's essential to get, and keep, weight under control.

Dog diets – consult your vet to check your dog is healthy, apart from being too fat; if he isn't, then your vet will advise on the best diet and exercise plan. Otherwise, simply gradually reduce your dog's daily food intake to the appropriate level (see pages 92–93).

Treats – where both fussy and fat dogs are concerned, keep treats to a minimum and include them as part of the daily ration, not on top of it. Aim to wean your dog onto healthy treats, such as raw carrot and other vegetables. Consult a canine nutrition expert as to what fruit and vegetables are safe.

Begging for food

Ignore this behaviour for the sake of your dog's waistline and domestic harmony – a dog who whines at the table and attempts to steal food soon becomes a nuisance. See pages 112–113 for how to teach your dog table manners.

Food for treats and training

Food is extremely useful to use as training incentives and rewards, because many dogs will do anything for a tasty treat. You can buy commercially prepared treats in all shapes and flavours, or make your own. Once you have identified your pet's favourite, you'll have an excellent training tool.

Colours and flavours – choose commercial treats with as few artificial ingredients as possible, as these can cause behavioural and/or health problems in some dogs.

Calorie intake
Count any food treats given as part of your pet's ration.

Nature's best – get your dog used to having fresh fruit and vegetables as treats from a young age. Apples, green vegetables and young carrots make great treats, as do hotdog sausages cut up small and cooked offal, such as liver. See 'DIY training treats', below.

Ready supply – keep little pieces of treats in your pocket, or in an easily accessible bag at your waist, so that they are instantly to hand when required.

Earn the reward – always make your dog work for a treat, don't just give him one. Your dog will enjoy the game of working for his treat, as well as eating the reward, and it maintains training on a regular basis.

DIY training treats

375 g (12 oz) ox or lamb's liver
1.5 litres (2½ pints) cold water

1 Put the liver in a pan with the water and bring to the boil, then simmer until cooked (about 30 minutes).

2 Drain the water and when cool store in the fridge to add to regular mixer meals.

3 Preheat the oven to 140°C (275°F) Gas Mark 1. Grease a baking sheet or use a non-stick one.

4 Allow the liver to cool, then cut into small 1-cm (½-inch) pieces. Place on the prepared baking sheet and bake for about 1 hour, or until cooked through.

5 Allow to cool and use as required. Store in the fridge and use within 3 days.

Simple training solutions

Training a dog is pretty easy really – there's no mystery to it whatsoever, providing you stick to the ground rules of being fair, patient, self-controlled, calm, positive, consistent, understanding and clear in your directions and requirements from your pet. The main thing to realize is that reward plays the main part in successful obedience training, so stock up on treats and toys.

Praise and reward

When training them, dogs learn to associate a word with an action, so be aware of what your physical expression as well as your voice is telling him. For example, if you are encouraging him to come to you, make your body language as welcoming as your voice.

Start right – it's a good idea to find a good instructor, since being shown hands-on how to train your dog makes life easier for both of you. Attend a class once a week initially. Once you've got the hang of it, return for refresher lessons when required.

Short and sweet – keep training sessions brief and end on a good note, even if it means going back a step. This way your dog

remembers only positive associations with training sessions and will enjoy them and be eager to please. Never raise your voice in anger at your dog as this will only make him scared of you and be counter-productive.

Lots of praise – verbal praise should be delivered in a calm voice, to avoid undue excitability that you may find hard to calm or channel appropriately afterwards, and end on an encouraging and uplifting tone. Toy rewards should be those your dog enjoys playing with – keeping his most prized one as a high value treat for extra encouragement as necessary, or to gain extra attention and focus from him.

Learned response – rewarding your dog (with verbal praise and/or a food treat) every time he does as you wish on a word-action command leads to a learned response. Eventually that response will become

Key question
Should I reward with a food treat every time my dog displays desirable behaviour?
No, or he may put on too much weight. Once he's learned what actions are required of him, food treat at random to keep his response levels high.

automatic every time you say the command and display the action – similar to when you check your wrist when asked the time.

Check yourself – beware of rewarding undesirable behaviour or your dog will assume that his actions are acceptable. For example, if he dives into his food dish before you've had chance to put it down and this goes unchecked, then this action is a reward in itself. Train him to wait until the food is on the floor and he's given permission to eat.

Right on cue

Ever wondered why some dogs respond to their owners as if by magic when a quiet word, or a barely perceptible hand movement or body posture, is directed at them? Well, it's easy when you know how. Patience + perseverance + consistency = obedient pet.

Command words – choose ones that are easy for you to remember, roll off the tongue and are short, so more easily understandable for your dog, such as 'down', 'sit' and so forth.

Consistency – dogs respond best to calm and consistent actions and commands for desirable behaviours, but it's essential that all members of the family use the same commands and follow the code of training practice you instigate.

Verbal commands – these should be encouraging and given at an even pitch. Keep commands clear and well spaced (at least at first), so you don't confuse your dog.

Hand signal – these are also known as 'cues', train your dog to respond to these by putting a hand signal to go with the verbal cue (see right) so he learns to associate the signal with the spoken command.

No means no

If a displayed behaviour is unacceptable, such as pestering for attention, then a 'No' command given in a quiet but firm 'growl' from you, and turning your attention away from your dog, will teach him that such behaviour is unrewarding for him, so he usually won't bother to do it again.

Confusion – if your dog has learned to ignore a command, and probably thinks it means something else (such as you saying 'heel' when he's walking in front of you and pulling, so he associates 'heel' with pulling ahead), then use a different word to re-train him, such as 'side'. Teach one command at a time, waiting until your dog is fully au fait with it before progressing to another.

HAND SIGNALS AND VOICE COMMANDS

'Watch me'

'Over!'

'Sit'

'Close!'

'Down!'

'Here!'

'Stand'

'Stay!'

Lead training

Walking your dog everyday should be an enjoyable experience and basic lead training will ensure that you are in charge, rather than him taking you for a walk. Here's how to teach your dog that it feels good, and is rewarding, to wear a collar and walk by your side on a lead in a controlled manner – in a few simple steps. Start by getting him used to his collar before introducing the lead.

Collar training

- Initially, put the collar on your dog for short periods, praising him lavishly as you do so. Make sure it fits properly – you should be able to fit two fingers under it; if it's a half-check collar, there should be at least two chain links between the two D rings.
- Once the collar is on, distract him with a game or a treat so that he gets used to the feel of something around his neck and associates it with a rewarding experience.

- When your dog is at ease, clip on a short leash and let him follow you around for short periods.
- When he's happy with that exercise, start to encourage him to walk by your side while you hold the leash.

ON THE LEAD

1 Hold the leash in your right hand and a reward in your left to gain your dog's interest and attention. Walk backwards and call his name; keep the leash slack and entice him to you with the reward.

2 Once your dog is happily walking towards you, bring your reward hand around towards your left leg and then forward, and he will turn to follow it. Walk forwards, use the command 'heel' and reward him for staying with you.

3 The picture shows the correct way to hold the leash and the correct position for the dog by your side.

Key tip

During initial training, keep a toy or treat in your left hand so that if your dog is distracted, starts pulling or lags behind, you can entice him back to the correct position and pace, then reward him.

Walking to heel

Educating your dog to stay by your side while out walking, and come back to that position when called, is important. So the next step in obedience school is teaching him what the command 'heel' means. Only when your dog has learned where 'heel' is, can you use the command to bring him back to the position. Once he's learned to stay to heel on the lead, practise off-leash. Lots of rewards will reap dividends.

HEEL TRAINING

1 Begin with your dog on your left side and encourage him into position by your left leg with a tasty treat, or a toy. Say his name to gain his attention and when you have it, say 'heel'.

Key tip
Keep treats or a toy in your pocket, then your dog is more likely to remain by your side in the heel position – just in case a reward comes his way.

2 Begin walking forwards purposefully, say 'come'. Say 'heel' when he is in the required position and after a couple of steps, stop and reward him. This is so that he learns the word by association with the position he's in when he gets the reward. Hold a treat in your left hand so he can see it and stays close to you in the hope of getting it. Don't walk too fast for him to keep up.

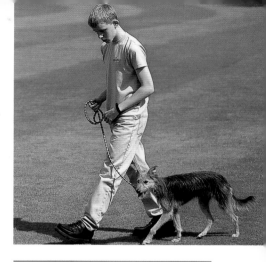

3 If he lags behind or pulls in front of you, don't say 'heel' to return him to the position as it will confuse him. Stop, and he will probably look back in surprise.

4 Guide him back into position, using rewards as necessary to get his attention again, as in Stage 1. Begin walking again. Repeat Stages 1–4 as necessary and your dog will soon get the idea.

Simple training solutions **107**

Road safety

Calmness and obedience from your dog while you are walking beside roads is essential for everyone's safety. It's even more important that he comes back to you should you let go of the lead for some reason, or it breaks, and he inadvertently becomes unattached from you (see pages 122–123 for instant, obedient recall training).

Vital safety – knowing how to cross a road correctly with your dog is essential. There is an obvious danger in an owner struggling across a road with a dog who is out of control. Accustom your dog to traffic on quiet roads at first, distracting him with rewards so that he learns that traffic is good, not bad.

Sit! – in order to cross a road safely, your dog must obey the 'sit' command (see pages 114–115). Only when he is sitting calmly by your side can you fully concentrate on the traffic to be sure the road is clear before you cross.

Stop, look and listen – when crossing a road, stop at a point where you have a good view in both directions. Avoid crossing at corners and junctions, unless there is a pedestrian crossing.

Before crossing – command your dog to sit at the heel position before stepping into the road. Continue to remind your dog to stay, keeping his attention on you with a treat, toy or verbal encouragement until you cross.

Safe crossing – cross only when the road is clear in both directions. Keep checking for approaching vehicles and keep your dog's attention on you by having a reward in the hand closest to him.

Key question
What type of lead is best suited to walking on roads?

A fixed length lead is best. Using a retractable lead isn't a good idea when walking your dog next to traffic. If he dashes out into the path of a vehicle you may not be able to reel him in quickly enough. Always keep him on a lead when on or near roads.

Teaching patience

Dogs that demand your attention all the time, as and when they want it, can be both irritating and draining. So teach your dog to respect your space – as you do his – by being patient and undemanding, in three simple steps.

BE PATIENT

Key tip

Be consistent – if you allow your dog to behave in a certain way one day, and not the next, he will end up confused and frustrated. Lay down one set of rules for acceptable and desirable behaviour and actions and always stick to them.

1 Don't allow your dog to demand your attention whenever he wants it. If he does, maybe by jumping up or pawing at you, gently push him away.

2 Ignore him until he stops bothering you and remains quiet.

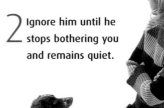

Pushy pets

Every year dogs tripping up or pushing over their owners cause many accidents, especially among elderly people. Dogs that push in front of you through doorways and down steps, and generally barge about getting under your feet, need to be taught not to do this for safety's sake. Here's how:

- Teach your dog to sit and stay (see pages 114–117).

- Put stair-gates at the top and bottom of the stairs to prevent your dog running up and down them until he's learned not to do this until invited.
- Make him wait calmly and obediently until you invite him to go through doors in a safe and controlled manner.
- If he lies in doorways, don't step over him and risk losing your footing and hurting yourself – direct him to move.

3 Now you can reward him for being patient and undemanding. Through the use of vocal and physical (petting) reward, and food motivation as required, your dog will learn that he'll get attention when you want to give it to him and not when he demands it.

Table manners

If you don't mind your dog begging for food at your mealtimes, are happy to give him suitable scraps and this doesn't cause any problems for you, then that's absolutely fine. If, however, you find it a nuisance and it's leading to undesirable behaviour, then you need to teach him not to do it.

Cleanliness – it's not really ideal to allow dogs in the kitchen for hygiene's sake, but this room is actually where they are often kept. This being the case, it's important they are taught not to jump up and lick food preparation and serving surfaces.

Table titbits – while it can be tempting to give your dog scraps from your plate at the table, avoid doing so as it will encourage him to hover near you, and then beg for more. Make sure everyone in the house abides by this rule. Put suitable human food scraps in his food dish instead and give these at his set mealtimes.

Disappearing food – children especially, should be told not to feed dogs at the table, as they do tend to do this (especially when your back is turned and they don't like certain foods – as there's nowhere better to hide them than in the dog!).

Deterring begging tips

There are several steps you can take:

- Remove your dog from the room while you are preparing food and eating.
- If your dog responds to being directed to go away and lie down and stay quietly, then do this when you sit down to eat. When you've finished you can reward and 'release' him. This way he learns that leaving you alone at the table is rewarding for him.
- Allowing your dog to lick plates may lead him to, naturally, associate this as the norm and think that plated meals are for him, which can result in stealing from the table and begging for food as you are eating.
- Giving food scraps to your dog when preparing meals often results in teaching your dog to 'hound' you while you prepare meals, so avoid doing it.

Sit

Being able to get your dog to sit down on command is the basic starting point for further training, such as 'lie down' and 'stay'. The key to teaching your dog to sit is patience, as dogs initially feel vulnerable in this position.

ACER – four principles apply to sit training (and also to teaching your dog to walk to heel, see pages 106–107) and you can easily remember them via the acronym ACER (**A**ttention; **C**ommand; **E**xecute; **R**eward). Here's how you do it:

Attention – stand with your dog on your left, with the lead and a treat or toy in your right hand. Get his attention by saying his name.

Command – give the command – 'sit' – and simultaneously apply gentle pressure with

Key question

I've heard that using a clicker is a good way of teaching required actions. What is a clicker and how does it work?

A clicker is a small hand-held tool used to 'condition' desirable behaviour. You simply click as soon as the dog displays a required behaviour and reward him with a food treat. This way he learns that a click means reward; no click means no reward. You can also use it at a distance from your dog and he will come to you for his expected reward.

For example, to clicker-train 'sit':
1 Stand with your dog and wait until he sits.
2 As soon as he does, click and say 'sit' (and/or use a hand signal).
3 Reward him with a treat and praise.

your left hand on to your dog's rear end to push him down.

Execute – responding to the pressure of your hand, your dog will execute the command by sitting.

Reward – when he does, immediately reward him with the treat or toy and verbal praise. It's as simple as that.

Stay

Being able to get your dog to stay where you want him, indoors and out, is extremely useful. For instance, use this command if you have visitors and want him to remain in his bed, or if he needs to stay put for safety's sake while out on a walk.

Free stay

Once you are happy that your dog will stay put on the stay command on the long line, you can progress to the free stay. To do this, put him in the sit position and move away from him, command 'stay' and drop the line on the floor. Wait a few seconds, then walk back to and around your dog, finishing by his right hand side. Reward him.

STAY TRAINING

1 Using a long training line (gathered up initially), put your dog in the sit position by your left heel.

2 Take one step out to the side of him and command 'stay'. Hold your right hand palm open in front of him as a visual signal to stay put.

3 Repeat 'stay' and walk around the front of him slowly, with the line slack and still operating your hand cue. Stay close to him so he knows where you are and that you are not leaving him.

4 When you complete your circuit around him you should finish on his right hand side. Reward him with calm, gentle praise and a treat.

5 Repeat the exercise, gradually moving further away in front of him but coming in close round the back.

6 As your dog becomes confident you are not abandoning him, develop the stay further by extending the line and move further away from him as you walk all around him.

7 To free your dog from stay, say his name and then 'here', encouraging him to come to you. Reward him when he does so.

Leave it alone

Sometimes you'll want your pet to leave things alone for all sorts of reasons (such as food, other pets, toys, household objects and animal droppings), so it's vital that he recognizes and respects the command to do so. Start by teaching him to leave his food, then apply the same principles to other things.

Food training – using food is an effective way to teach your dog to leave something alone. Begin by having him on a lead and put down his food bowl. Do not allow him to eat, using the lead to restrain him as necessary, along with the command 'leave'. Direct him to sit (see pages 114–115), or stand, quietly.

Wait and stay – while your dog is waiting to eat, move away from him and use the command 'wait' or 'stay', which he will do because he is unwilling to move away from the food.

Permission to eat – wait until your dog looks at you for permission to eat. Eventually he'll look to you to see whether you are ready to let him eat. When he does, say, encouragingly, 'eat' and let him do so. Praise him for being obedient and patient.

Treat him – while he is eating, add a treat or more food to his bowl so that he views hands near his dinner as non-threatening. This way you are also teaching him not to be possessive over items he sees as his. Do this exercise every mealtime until your dog will wait off lead until given permission to eat.

Under control – once your dog understands the routine where food is concerned, use the 'leave' command to teach your dog to leave other things alone and to stay and wait where you want him.

Key tip

Supervise children in the household to carry out 'leave' training to help prevent the dog taking toys that are not his, but never let them tease the dog by withholding food unfairly or for too long.

Down boy

Teaching your dog to lie down and stay in that position until you say otherwise is useful for lots of things, such as when the vet wants to check him over, for grooming and for just having him lie quietly while you are occupied with something else.

TEACHING THE 'DOWN' COMMAND

1 With your dog in the sit position (see pages 114–115), get him to focus his attention on a treat in your hand.

2 Put the treat under his nose, then, slowly, move it down to the floor between his front legs

Lie and stay – if all goes well, try extending the down exercise into a stay. Step away from your dog, saying 'stay' as you do so. Wait for a couple of seconds, go back to him and reward him. Gradually increase the distance between you and your dog as you command the stay.

Stand up – getting your dog to sit up and then stand from a lying position is quite easy. Simply put a treat under his nose and raise it above his head, simultaneously saying 'sit' or 'stand'. Reward him for the desired response with a treat and praise.

Multi-tasking – practise all three exercises until your dog understands each one. Then request a sit, a down and a stay, and reward him when he does the required action. Finally, request all of these and then a stand after the stay, then reward. This usually turns out to be a game that a dog enjoys.

Key fact
Instant reward and lots of confidence-giving praise is essential when teaching the down exercise because dogs feel vulnerable in a lying position.

3 He'll sink to the floor in his effort to get hold of the reward. As soon as he does, say 'down' and when his elbows rest on the ground, let him have the treat and give him lots of praise.

Come back

A dog that won't come back to you when you call his name is not only annoying, he's a liability, too. So for safety's sake, he needs to be obedient to recall as and when you want him.

Reward incentive – initially, the reward should be of high value, such as a really tasty treat or a prized toy. Lots of praise is also beneficial – an enthusiastic and rewarding welcome from you will encourage him to recall.

Conditioned rewards – as your dog becomes conditioned to return to you on command, praise will probably be sufficient. You can, however, give occasional high-value rewards to maintain instant response.

TEACHING RECALL

1 To begin, walk forward with your dog on a long leash and at heel as usual. Then allow the leash to go slack and move backwards, calling your dog's name and the command 'come' at the same time. Offer a treat or high-value toy to elicit a quick response.

2 As the dog reaches you, say 'sit', and when he responds give the treat or play a game with a toy and praise him lavishly.

3 Once he is responding instantly each time you do this exercise, try dropping the leash on the ground (within easy reach in case you need to grab it) to see what his reaction is. When you are happy that he will come to you immediately on command, try the exercise off-leash in a secure area, gradually increasing the distance between you.

4 Finish on a success. If the dog recalls the first time, end the lesson there, leaving him with a positive association. If you have difficulties teaching this obedience, consult a professional trainer. It is vital that your dog instantly comes back on command when you need him to.

House manners

It is important that your dog understands his place in the household and behaves appropriately. Mutual respect is essential for harmonious living together and safe interaction, therefore ground rules must be laid so your dog knows what is, and isn't, allowed.

House rules – be consistent with house rules and commands; not letting him do something one day and then allowing it the next may result in a confused dog displaying stress and anxiety induced behaviours, such as chewing, toileting inside or even showing aggression.

Greeting visitors – if you do not want your dog to meet home visitors by jumping up at them and continually pestering them for attention, teach him not to via the sit/stay, leave and down commands (see pages 114–117, 118–119 and 120–121).

Possessiveness – if your dog is possessive over things, such as his bed, toys and food and growls or snaps if anyone goes near them, then, for safety's sake, only give him these things under safe supervision. Seek professional hands-on help as a priority.

Overenthusiastic welcome – if your dog leaps all over you on your return home and you don't want him to, then you need to re-educate him not to do this. Simply enter, do

Happy families

Teaching your pet how to behave acceptably in the home and in relation to humans in the household, and visitors, will lead to a more harmonious and comfortable existence for you both. Failing to do this leads, unfortunately, to a dog being reprimanded for behaving only as he's been taught, so you owe it to him to learn how to handle dogs correctly before owning one, or at least ensure you and your dog attend training classes on a regular basis to keep you both on the right track.

what you need to and ignore him. Only acknowledge him when he settles down, then he learns that a quiet welcome from him is more rewarding.

On your lap – only let your dog sit beside you, or on your lap, if invited to do so. Teach him to stay on the floor, unless you specifically ask him to join you on the sofa. Teach him to get down on command also.

Out of sight, out of mind – keep waste bins and other items you do not want your dog to interfere with securely out of his way, thereby avoiding temptation and potential conflict.

Training older dogs

Older dogs can learn obedience just like younger ones – the training principles are the same – but it may take time and patience to break undesirable ingrained habits. Oldies enjoy training games and it helps to keep them mentally alert.

Unreal expectations – if you've just taken on an older dog, don't expect him to automatically know what is required of him. He has to get to know you and your way of doing things, while you have to get to know him and find out what makes him tick.

Golden oldies – mature dogs may not hear or see too well, so don't assume he is ignoring you when you ask him to do something. Have his sight and hearing checked out by a vet to see how well these senses are functioning.

Slow but sure – if physical fitness and agility isn't 100 per cent, then take things slower with your dog and don't ask too much of him.

Short sessions – doing too much in one session will over-tax the dog both mentally and physically and he may end up confused. Keep it short and interspersed with play sessions for light relief and reward. Ten to 15 minutes of training per hour is the maximum most dogs can cope with.

Size matters – some dogs, particularly small ones, learn things faster than others. This is because smaller dogs, such as Yorkshire Terriers and Jack Russells, mature mentally and physically earlier than large breeds.

Key fact
Working breeds, such as a Boxer or Springer Spaniel, have an inbred instinct to chase and retrieve, guard or herd, and require disciplined handling and training to get the best from them.

No contact? – if your older dog hasn't been socialized properly then find a training school that holds socialization classes for 'oldies' in a safe and controlled environment.

Training progress – keep a diary so that you can see progress and note down areas of particular achievement or difficulty.

Resolving training problems

There may be occasions when you seem to come up against a brick wall when training, and your dog doesn't seem to know what you require of him. The key is to look at the problem, consider possible reasons for it and come up with an alternative solution.

Professional help – often the easiest and quickest way of successful training is to consult a professional trainer and have them show (and not just tell) you what techniques to use effectively.

Combating confusion – ensure everyone who comes in contact with your dog follows your rules for him, otherwise you may end up with one bewildered pet. It is especially important to instruct children on how to give commands.

Not guilty – never blame the dog. If he does something 'wrong', it's because he has not been taught how to do it right consistently. Dogs are incapable of feeling guilty as humans do. A 'guilty' expression is one of apprehension and fear of expected punishment due to a human's body language and tone of voice.

Think positive – however frustrated you feel, keep positive and offer lots of praise to your dog. He needs to see you as a source of comfort and security rather than fear or worry.

Soiling inside – there are reasons for 'accidents' in the house. For example, a dog may have been left inside too long and had no choice, or he was not toilet-trained to go outside correctly. He may be suffering illness, or fright (such as during a thunderstorm or fireworks being set off).

Start again – in most cases, going back to the beginning of training procedures to reaffirm them works successfully. Trying something different, such as agility training, can also help resolve behaviour and training difficulties.

Key fact

A rescue dog may find the stay command difficult to learn because he may feel he is being abandoned. If this is the case, then be patient with him and don't ask this of him until he realizes that you are not leaving him.

Problem behaviours

Sometimes your dog may display behaviours that you find unacceptable or upsetting, and which are disruptive to your family life. A question that dog trainers hear all the time is 'Why does my dog misbehave?' Read on to find out why dogs do certain things – and how to positively resolve problem behaviours satisfactorily.

Why dogs misbehave

The main reason why dogs 'misbehave' is because they've been forced into behaving that way by humans failing to train and stimulate them sufficiently. It is important, however, before embarking on a re-training programme, that you get your dog checked out by a vet to ensure there is no physical reason for the problem behaviour(s).

Natural behaviour – left to their own devices, dogs interact mostly equably among themselves by establishing a pecking order and rules. Dogs in a human world learn by association, and behave in a way that is most rewarding to them and to also maintain self-preservation. For example, if you allow a dog to do something one day which he finds rewarding and not the next and is reprimanded for attempting to do so, he becomes confused as to how he should act and behave, which can lead to him using aggressive behaviour in order to fend off your presence and preserve his rewarding resources (such as sitting on the sofa, for example). See pages 140–141.

Misread signals – is your dog really misbehaving, or is he doing what he thinks is the right thing? Instead of being annoyed at your dog, look at ways to improve the situation via correct, consistent and positive training.

Inbred behaviours – some dogs, particularly in working and herding breeds, do things we find unpleasant or aggressive (such as chasing smaller animals, or nipping ankles), but that is what they were bred to do. They need clear direction to channel their instincts in positive and acceptable ways.

Lazy owners – once a dog has learned the basics and achieved a good level of obedience and acceptable behaviour, some owners become complacent and fail

Key fact

The key to all successful corrective training is not to get angry, which could exacerbate a situation, but show him an alternative behaviour that is more rewarding for everyone.

to maintain consistency in direction, hence why 'misbehaviours' creep in.

Quick response – problem behaviours usually become worse if not dealt with appropriately and quickly. Always be consistent in your training and show your dog who is in control.

Help that works – occasionally, there is no quick-fix solution where some behavioural problems are concerned, such as aggression and chasing other animals. Enlist the advice and help of a professional canine behaviourist or trainer who can prove they have had success in this field. You should be told as well as shown how to deal with situations in situ.

Problem behaviours

A happy balance

To keep your dog amenable, happy and obedient you need to balance training, affection, rest and play in equal measures, since one or two without the others may lead to problem behaviours developing. Familiarize yourself with his needs and see how best to respond to achieve a mutually respectful relationship.

A BALANCING ACT

Canine Needs	Human Actions
Approach	Avoid sudden movements or loud noises directed at your dog, which he might construe as an aggressive threat
Reward	Always reward good behaviour
Food and drink	Feed your dog a suitable diet in the correct daily quantity for his size and energy requirements (see pages 92–93)
Attention and exercise	Lots of daily affection and playtime is necessary, as well as sufficient exercise on and off-lead and social interaction with his own kind
Health care	Have your pet vaccinated against common diseases and treat him as necessary for parasites (see pages 158–159). Seek veterinary attention if you think he may be ill, be suffering discomfort or is displaying unusual behaviour
Understanding	If he displays natural behaviours, such as rolling in animal droppings, don't reprimand him for it. Simply distract him with a toy or food treat
Possessions	Provide your dog with toys to play with so he's less likely to take or chew other items in the house
Companionship	To deny a dog human company for long periods is unfair and can lead to problem behaviour
Elimination	Give a dog an area where he knows he can relieve himself, and clean up after him
Safety	Don't put your dog in situations that are hazardous or make him uneasy
Space	Dogs are quick to sense their owners' emotions and can be upset when all is not well. He needs his own private space (den) to retreat to and feel secure in when needed
Rest	His den should also be a place where your dog can rest and relax when he needs to without being disturbed
Discipline	Don't use aggressive vocal or physical chastisement or a dog may retaliate in kind. Employ positive redirection instead

Chase control

Dogs that chase after other dogs, animals and even people are a liability. Often this behaviour is a playful 'practise-pursuit' due to a dog's instinct to run after and catch anything that moves. You need to stop, or at least be able to control this behaviour. Listed below are a few solutions.

No prompting – never encourage a dog to chase any animal, such as cats, out of the garden. Unchecked, dogs find chasing a rewarding pastime, but you need to re-train him to think that it is not, otherwise it can lead to unpleasant, even fatal, consequences.

Expert help – it is important to enlist a professional and experienced trainer to help you remove your dog's chase tendencies, since it is unlikely you will be able to resolve it alone.

Disc-training – this can be useful in discouraging a 'chaser', but you must be taught how to do this correctly. Find a trainer who is experienced in using discs and other chase-deterrent effective training aids, particularly in serious chase cases.

Socializing – when this is done gradually it may prove useful, providing there is no risk or stress to other people or animals involved.

Firm focus – the most important factor in re-training a 'chaser' is to keep his attention firmly on you and be sure that he understands and instantly responds to the heel (pages 106–107), stay (pages 116–117)

Key question
What is disc-training?
Disc-training employs the use of small metal discs on a string that rattle if shaken or thrown close to the dog to discourage undesirable behaviour(s), but it should only be done by someone who fully understands how and when to use them and back them up with appropriate handling and training, otherwise it won't work and more harm than good can be achieved if used incorrectly.

and recall (pages 122–123) commands. Maintain his attention with high-value (his favourite) toys and treats.

Under control – do not let a 'chaser' off the lead in public places, or where there's livestock, until re-training is firmly established and you are absolutely sure you have full control of your dog. Keep him on an extending lead or long line while re-training so that you have control at all times.

Destructive tendencies

Dogs like to chew things and don't know what's off the menu unless you teach them what they are allowed to chew, and what they are not. Without guidance, a destructive dog can soon wreck a house, and cost you a fortune.

Preventative measures – until your dog learns that your belongings are off the menu, never leave things lying around that you don't want destroyed.

Keep him occupied – chewing gives a dog a lot of pleasure, particularly if he is bored, so keeping him busy is the best way to keep your home intact (see pages 134–135).

Home alone – if you are out for long periods and your dog starts chewing things to ward off loneliness and boredom, take him to a dog-sitter or ask a friend or neighbour to pop by and check on him.

Purpose-made – provide your dog with alternatives to the things you don't want him to chew that will be just as rewarding to him and more acceptable to you. This will teach him that he can only chew certain items that you give him for that purpose, such as chew toys and food chews. Tough rubber chew toys filled with treats should have two holes in them for safety.

Restricted areas – until he's been re-trained not to destroy 'forbidden' things, restrict your dog to an area where he can't do any

damage when you are unable to keep an eye on him. Give him chew and activity toys to keep him occupied. Conditioning him to chew these items will take his mind off chewing unacceptable items.

Taste aversion – reinforce, if necessary, that certain items, such as shoes, are unpleasant for him to chew by spraying them with non-toxic anti-chew liquid. This tastes so vile that your dog won't be keen to go back for a second helping after his first taste and will find a toy that is much nicer to chew on.

Lost objects

Swallowing objects, like bits of chewed toys, shoe laces and clothing, such as socks or gloves, can lead to intestinal blockages which result in pain and, often, expensive surgery to remove them. Blockages can prove fatal in some cases.

Aggression

There is always a reason for aggression in a dog, who uses it as self-preservation when they think they are under threat. However, this behaviour is unacceptable in human society so it must be dealt with practically and swiftly, in order that no one is hurt. There are many different reasons for aggression to develop, and several options available for how to deal with it, depending on its severity.

Professional help

Seek professional help as a matter of urgency if your dog is aggressive, you cannot cope with it and other people/animals are at risk from your pet. A good trainer will come out to you to assess you and your dog in your home environment. They will be able to ascertain what is causing the aggressive behaviour and thereby be able to suggest and demonstrate ways of dealing with, and solving, the problem quickly and effectively before you lose confidence, enabling the dog to become even more difficult to handle and someone is hurt.

Acquired behaviour – no dog is born aggressive, they learn to be through situation and circumstances, which include fear and anxiety, unclear signals that lead to confusion, aggression towards them, and possessiveness.

Self-preservation – a lack of socialization and consistent, correct, training is usually the root cause. If a dog learns that being aggressive is rewarding to him in some way, then this is how he will behave. If, say, he snaps when you try to get him off the sofa so you leave him, that is rewarding to him.

Guarding – by growling and/or snapping at anyone, or another animal, that approaches a particular object – be it a bowl of food, a toy or even its human pack-mate – is a dog's way of saying 'this is mine and you cannot have it'.

Age training – teach dogs from a young age to relinquish items without a fuss (see pages 54–55). Curing the habit in an older dog is often more difficult – as well as scary and painful sometimes – so you need to get expert hands-on help, fast!

Immediate action – many dogs who bite either humans or other animals don't get a chance to be reformed for reasons of human safety and perhaps the possibility of future litigation, and may be taken away from their owners. A trainer who is experienced in dealing with aggression cases will advise whether removal or appropriate training is in order.

Training option – this depends on all the circumstances involved, not least whether the owner is capable of and willing to follow advice given regarding the training option. And whether they can afford it in terms of time, money and risk.

Nervous dogs

Some dogs can be more sensitive, or nervous, than others – even if you cannot see a reason for it. More understandably, so are many dogs that have suffered mental and/or physical abuse or neglect. Whatever the cause, you can do much to ease an anxious dog's worry.

Reassurance signs – just like some people, some dogs are more shy and retiring than others. Send out relaxed signals to a nervous dog, such as yawning or slow blinking. Ignore him if he gets anxious and behave as normally as possible, but not overly boisterously or noisily, so that your body language tells him 'It's all ok, there's nothing to worry about.'

Breed sensitivity – certain breeds, for example Rough Collies, Whippets, Shetland Sheepdogs, are known to be nervous of, and sensitive to, elements that are not right in

Scenting success

A nervous or anxious dog may respond to a dog-appeasing pheromone (DAP) diffuser spray or collar, which are available from pet stores and vets. Similar to a slow-release air freshener, the plug-in diffuser releases a synthetic copy of a dog's pacifying pheromones that are produced by a lactating female. A spray version is also available, which is ideal for use when travelling. Use DAP for:

- Fear of fireworks or loud noises
- Separation anxiety
- Chewing or destruction when home alone
- Barking
- House soiling
- Travel stress or car sickness

their world, such as their owner's ill temper or depressed mood. This can sometimes be due to a fear of certain things (see pages 146–147).

Rescue dogs – going into a new home can be scary for a dog and he'll take time to adjust. Allow for this, but avoid overly cosseting him. Taking a nervous dog to a suitable socialization class can help him to gain confidence.

Safe place – your dog must have a den that he can retreat to undisturbed for 'sanctuary'. Let him come to you, and other people, in his own time rather than force attention on him.

Security – ensuring your home is a nice and safe place to be for your dog, and that the humans in his life are friendly and kind, will help him relax, enjoy himself and gain confidence.

Separation anxiety

Being pack animals, dogs dislike being on their own as they feel vulnerable. Being alone affects some more than others, especially those that have a high dependency on their owners or who have previously been abandoned. Separation anxiety manifests in various undesirable behaviours such as destructiveness and soiling inside the house.

Over-dependency – it is better for the dog that you do not encourage him to become over-dependent as it will lead to problems when you need to leave him on his own.

It is not fair on a dog to encourage him to be so highly dependent on you that he cannot let you out of sight without feeling anxious.

Home alone – for a dog to remain mentally and physically healthy, being alone for long periods while his owner is at work is not the best environment. Get around this by taking him to a dog-sitter or kennels, or arrange for someone reliable to come in to see to your dog when you are out.

Panic attacks – a common problem in old dogs is 'geriatric separation anxiety', which usually becomes apparent at night when everyone is asleep. The dog wakes, feels disorientated and doesn't know where his owners are. He barks, pants, is very anxious and may even soil. Veterinary treatment can help resolve these panic attacks.

Attention-seeking – older dogs often get more clingy and display an increased need for human company. Leaving a radio on low can help reassure him when you are out for short periods, as can giving him treat-filled activity toys to occupy him.

Pheromone treatment – a DAP diffuser (see page 142) can prove helpful in reducing anxiety in your dog. Plug it in near his bed or den.

Alternative therapy
In some cases, herbal rescue remedies, such as Bach Flower Rescue Remedy, have been found to be effective in alleviating separation (and general) anxiety. Pop a couple of drops on your dog's tongue an hour or so before you go out. Seek veterinary advice before administering.

Problem behaviours

Fears and phobias

Like some humans, some dogs have a fear or phobia about certain things such as loud noises from thunder or fireworks, rolled up newspapers and sticks, but there are ways to ease fears and overcome phobias.

Overly sensitive

If your dog shows extreme fear at loud noises, have his hearing checked out in case he's hypersensitive to noise.

FEARS AND SOLUTIONS

Phobia	Cause	Solution
Fear of objects	If a dog has had a bad experience with a certain object, such as being hit with a rolled-up newspaper or a stick, then he associates those things with pain	Leave the objects lying around the house to de-sensitize him to them; reward him for going near them. Work towards picking up the objects and call your dog to you while you hold them, reassuring and rewarding him, so he learns to associate them with good things
Fear of vehicles	The size and noise and speed of traffic worries some dogs, usually because they have not been acclimatized to it properly, or due to being hit by a vehicle	Gradually acclimatize him to traffic on quiet roads, both day and night, offering lots of treats to distract him and so that he associates traffic with reward. To be on the safe side, ensure your dog is always on a lead when walking on public highways
Fear of thunder or fireworks	Loud noise can hurt a dog's ears. One train of thought is that dogs view thunderstorms as dangerous because of lightning strikes	Keep the dog inside and ensure he has a covered den where he can feel safe. Food-filled activity toys will distract and occupy him. Avoid fussing him as this will reinforce his fear. Noise de-sensitization CDs can help, as can leaving the radio or television on. A DAP diffuser may help alleviate fear, as may rescue remedies (see page 145) and a soothing massage

Out and about

One of the best things about owning a dog is getting out and about on walks with him in both urban areas and the countryside. There's so much to see and do together – and you can even take him on holiday with you since there are many pet-friendly places to stay and visit.

Travelling with your dog

It's lovely to be able to include your dog in everyday life and there's nothing more pleasant than a family outing to the park or beach. For many, this involves a trip in the car and there are several things you should do to help make the journey comfortable and safe.

Safe travel – transport your dog in a travel crate. This will prevent him from distracting you while you are driving, and also helps to keep him safe and secure in the event of an accident.

Crate bedding – put some non-slip flooring in the crate, such as a rubber mat, with his bedding on top. Alternatives to a crate are a strong, well-ventilated pet carrier (for small dogs) or a dog grille. You can also get canine travel harnesses.

Precious cargo – keeping the car well ventilated is essential, as is driving with consideration. Keep gear changes and cornering smooth and braking gradual, so your dog isn't flung around in his crate – motion sickness can be aggravated by jerky and erratic driving, fast cornering and sudden braking. There is a prescription medication available especially for motion sickness without making your dog drowsy.

Pit stops – ensure you make regular stops for exercise and comfort breaks on long journeys. Park in a safe area and keep your dog on his lead.

Key travel tips
- To help avoid vomiting, don't feed your dog immediately before a trip
- Never leave your dog unattended in the car. Dogs can become overheated in a short time, which is potentially fatal
- Let your dog toilet before a journey
- Take water and a bowl with you on a day trip
- Pack cleaning cloths, plastic bags and disinfectant so you can deal with any sickness or soiling
- Covering the crate with a blanket can help quieten noisy travellers

Doggy sleepovers

Whether travelling for a long weekend or a family holiday, taking your dog with you makes the holiday complete. There are a few things to remember before you leave:

- Check out pet-friendly accommodation options in the area you intend to visit well in advance

- If travelling abroad, ensure your pet has a passport if required and is up to date with any vaccinations
- Pack crate and bedding
- Feeding and water bowls
- Food
- Favourite toys and treats
- Lead and collar
- Canine first aid kit (see page 162)

Problems on a walk

Walking your dog should be a pleasurable experience for both of you, but sometimes problems can occur while you are out and about. Here's how to deal with common situations both quickly and effectively.

Pulling – a dog that pulls can make walks a trial, so re-educating him to stay at heel while on the lead is in order (see pages 106–107). Stopping and/or turning suddenly will help keep him alert and focused on you, as will smelly treats in your pocket closest to him. If you keep stopping when he pulls he learns that pulling gets him nowhere. Walking him in a canine head collar or a harness may solve the problem.

Slowcoaches – either you are walking too fast for your dog to keep up, or he's more interested in sniffing to identify who has been along that way previously, and possibly urinating to mark his own passage. In the first instance, slow down a bit; in the second use a reward to maintain his attention on you and encourage him to keep up, or simply insist he remains at heel.

Poor exercise tolerance – sometimes a normally active dog will develop problems that make exercise difficult for him and he may shows signs of pain and discomfort, such as sitting down often and limping, either during or after walks. Seek veterinary advice. In addition, there are some short-legged breeds that may find it difficult to maintain a brisk pace.

Old age – some elderly dogs may feel stiff and find walking long distances difficult. Bear this in mind, and only go as far as they are willing or able – never push them beyond their capabilities.

Stay alert – keep a watch out at all times on walks so you are prepared for all eventualities, such as your dog jumping up at passers-by or trying to run after another animal. Be aware that other dogs you meet may not be as well-trained and amenable as yours, so exercise caution when you encounter any off-leash. Ask a trainer how to deal with any potentially awkward situations.

IAM		EUKANUBA ADUL
IAM 14915	15 LB	EUKANUBA ADULT
IAM 27030	30 LB	EUKANUBA ADUL
IAM 27015	15 LB	EUKANUBA ADUL
IAM 03971	04 LB	EUKANUBA ADULT
IAM 01958	36 LB	EUKANUBA BREED
IAM 01953	36 LB	EUKANUBA BREED
IAM 01956	36 LB	EUKANUBA BREED S
IAM 02752	36 LB	EUKANUBA BREED S
IAM 00663	15 LB	EUKANUBA PUPPY L
IAM 04108	04 LB	EUKANUBA PUPPY L
IAM 60945	33 LB	EUKANUBA PUPPY L
IAM 04226	16.5LB	EUKANUBA PUPPY L
IAM 03984	05 LB	EUKANUBA PUPPY L

Page 2

Recall

If your dog won't come back to you instantly when off lead, re-educate him (see page 122), enlist hands-on training help and keep him on the lead or a long line until you've cured the problem. Loose, disobedient dogs are a liability.

Health care

Few things are lovelier to look at than a happy and healthy dog that is bright-eyed and full of vitality. Help keep him that way by watching and checking him over on a daily basis for signs of ailment so that you can catch and deal with it early, and ensuring you know what to do if illness or accidents occur. This section advises you how.

Routine procedures

Keeping your dog free of external and internal parasites, as well as having him vaccinated against canine diseases, is part and parcel of responsible and caring ownership.

Deadly diseases – many vets recommend that dogs are vaccinated against the four major, often fatal, canine diseases:

- Distemper virus
- Adenoviral hepatitis
- Canine parvovirus
- Leptospirosis

Coughs and colds – other vaccines are also available, including those against canine parainfluenza and *Bordetella bronchiseptica*. Vaccinations may be required for kennelling and showing.

When to vaccinate – to protect a dog properly against disease, he should have two lots of multiple vaccines – the first at 6–8 weeks old, and the second lot when he's at least 10 weeks old. The vaccines must be given 2–4 weeks apart. Booster vaccinations are given annually.

Rabies – in some countries, vaccinations for rabies are given routinely; in others, the vaccine is only necessary if you take your dog on holiday abroad.

Fleas – signs of fleas include agitation and scratching, with red and sore patches occurring. Fleas can also cause anaemia. The most effective treatments are 'spot-on' dispensers, oral treatments or via injection.

Worms – roundworms and tapeworms (the most common sort) cause all sorts of problems, including malnutrition and gut damage. Wormers usually come in tablet or powder form and can be administered in food. Worm regularly on veterinary advice.

Key fact

The best place to get effective applications that will kill fleas and worms is from your vet.

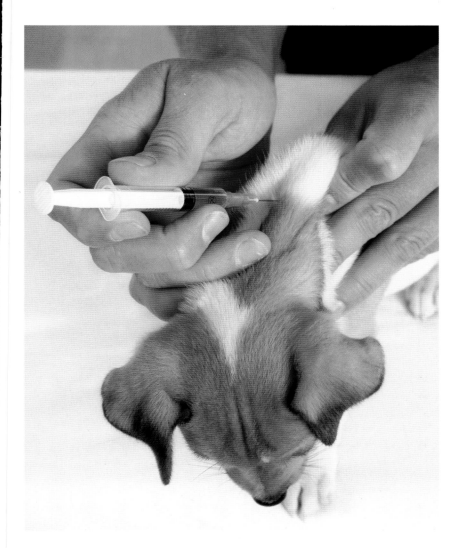

Signs of illness

Indications of illness are unusual behaviour, altered appetite or demeanour, distressed whining, increased or decreased thirst, straining on defecation or urination, vomiting or diarrhoea. Note if your dog displays any of these signs then you can inform the vet to help him diagnose what's wrong quickly so he can treat your pet appropriately.

Abnormal behaviour – it is important to recognize any changes from the norm in your dog's behaviour so that swift action or veterinary intervention can be taken. See the checklist opposite for key signs that all is not well.

Altered states – knowing your dog's normal TPR rates (vital signs) when well (see box, right), will alert you to any changes that may indicate illness.

When to call the vet – if you suspect that your dog is unwell, seek veterinary advice straight away as it's better to be safe than sorry. See pages 160–161 for some of the physical signs that can indicate whether you have a healthy or an unhealthy dog.

Abnormal behaviour checklist

- Depression
- Hyperactivity
- Distressed whining or barking
- Coughing or wheezing
- Limping
- A hunched up appearance or stance
- Increased thirst or hunger
- Incontinence
- Increased urination and/or defecation
- Abnormal coloured urine
- Constipation or loose motions
- Weight loss or gain
- Hair loss
- Unusual discharge
- Pain when touched
- Unusual aggression or timidity

Key question
How do I take my dog's TPR?

Monitor your dog's temperature, pulse and respiration (TPR) rates when he's relaxed and at rest on an average day (not too hot or cold), to discover what is normal for him.

- Taking temperature: the only sure way of ascertaining a dog's temperature is with a rectal thermometer. Ask your vet or vet nurse to show you how this is done before attempting it yourself.
- Taking pulse rate: make sure your dog is calm and resting. Lay him on his right side and place your hand over his chest, or locate the femoral artery on the inside of the thigh in the groin and press with your fingers, and count the heart beats for 15 seconds. Multiply this figure by four to obtain the heart rate per minute.

- Respiration can be measured by observing the flanks or by holding a wet finger or hand mirror, in front of the nostrils (then you can easily feel or see – via misting on the mirror – the exhaled breaths easily). Measure the respiration rate for 15 seconds, and then multiply by four to get the rate per minute.

A dog's normal vital signs of temperature, pulse and respiration (TPR) are:

Temperature 38.1–39.2°C (100.5–102.5°F)

Pulse 62–130 heart beats per minute (bpm); the smaller he is, the faster the pulse.

Respiration 10–30 breaths per minute; smaller dogs breathe faster.

SIGNS OF A HEALTHY DOG

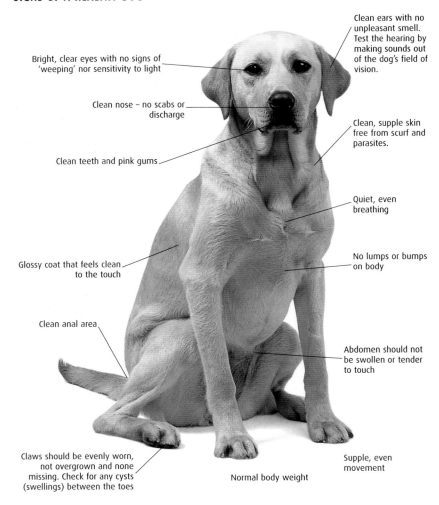

Clean ears with no unpleasant smell. Test the hearing by making sounds out of the dog's field of vision.

Bright, clear eyes with no signs of 'weeping' nor sensitivity to light

Clean nose – no scabs or discharge

Clean, supple skin free from scurf and parasites.

Clean teeth and pink gums

Quiet, even breathing

Glossy coat that feels clean to the touch

No lumps or bumps on body

Clean anal area

Abdomen should not be swollen or tender to touch

Claws should be evenly worn, not overgrown and none missing. Check for any cysts (swellings) between the toes

Supple, even movement

Normal body weight

SIGNS OF AN UNHEALTHY DOG

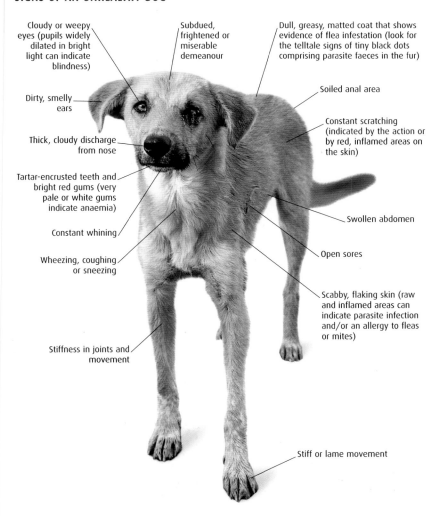

Cloudy or weepy eyes (pupils widely dilated in bright light can indicate blindness)

Dirty, smelly ears

Thick, cloudy discharge from nose

Tartar-encrusted teeth and bright red gums (very pale or white gums indicate anaemia)

Constant whining

Wheezing, coughing or sneezing

Stiffness in joints and movement

Subdued, frightened or miserable demeanour

Dull, greasy, matted coat that shows evidence of flea infestation (look for the telltale signs of tiny black dots comprising parasite faeces in the fur)

Soiled anal area

Constant scratching (indicated by the action or by red, inflamed areas on the skin)

Swollen abdomen

Open sores

Scabby, flaking skin (raw and inflamed areas can indicate parasite infection and/or an allergy to fleas or mites)

Stiff or lame movement

First aid

A knowledge of first aid is useful and, in some instances, essential if an emergency situation occurs so that you know what to do – and may even save your dog's life. Enrol on a canine first-aid course to learn how to treat minor ailments and cope in the event of an emergency.

Emergency first-aid – keep the dog in a safe restricted space, warm and quiet and consult your vet. Stem any bleeding by applying a clean pad to the area. Burns from fire or hot water should immediately be immersed in cold water for about 10 minutes. Do not pull out foreign objects – let a vet do that.

Wounds and bites – trim hair around the wound and clean it with saline solution and cotton wool. Apply antiseptic cream or other preparation as advised by your vet, to the area to help promote healing and protect against infection. Cut foot pads can be protected with a dog boot if necessary.

First-aid kit

- Thermometer
- Non-stick dressings
- Cotton wool
- Adhesive bandages
- A foot boot
- Open-weave bandages
- Saline solution
- Round-ended scissors
- Antiseptic cream and powder
- Liquid antiseptic
- Tweezers
- Lint and gauze
- Muzzle (in case your pet tries to bite you while you treat him)

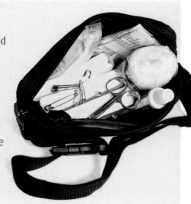

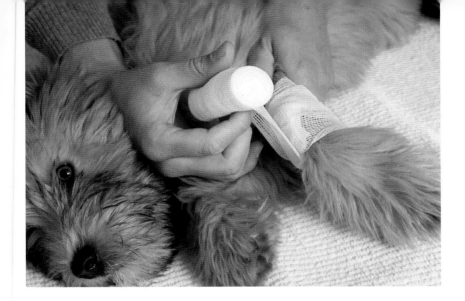

Stings – if you can see the sting, pull it out with tweezers. Wash wasp stings with vinegar and bee stings with a solution of water and bicarbonate of soda to neutralize the sting's effect.

Poisoning – symptoms of poisoning include excess salivation, sleepiness and/or signs of pain (crying, panting, restlessness), and fitting. If you suspect poisoning, call a vet immediately and follow their instructions: they may suggest making your dog sick and will give advice on how to do this, but will certainly tell you to bring your pet to the clinic as soon as you can.

Key question
What constitutes an emergency?
Consult a vet immediately if your dog is having breathing difficulties, suffers a snake bite, has broken something, is fitting, suffers sustained vomiting or diarrhoea, has abnormal vital signs (see page 161), is choking, has a foreign object lodged in his body, displays a stiff and/or unsteady gait, has been in an accident (traffic/drowning) or is suffering from heatstroke.

Stomach and skin problems

Digestive and skin disorders are the most common problems dog owners can face, but usually there's a simple solution. However, it's important to consult a vet in the first instance to gain a correct diagnosis and appropriate treatment plan.

Flatulence – try a change of diet to a better quality food, don't feed unsuitable table scraps, such as highly spiced or fatty food, and try to make your dog eat more slowly, thus reducing the amount of air swallowed.

Diarrhoea – sustained diarrhoea needs veterinary diagnosis to find the appropriate treatment. The cause can be a change of food, ingesting something unsuitable, a tummy bug or, more seriously, parvovirus.

Constipation – many diseases can cause this, but usually it's due to an unsuitable diet and lack of exercise. If the condition deteriorates and he's in discomfort, contact your vet.

Bloat – this can affect mainly large, deep-chested breeds, such as Great Danes and German Shepherds. Although the cause is uncertain, bloat comprises swelling and twisting of the stomach – and will be fatal within 60 minutes. Early signs include great discomfort and dry retching. Immediate veterinary attention and surgery is essential.

Seborrhoea – this comprises abnormal secretion from sebaceous glands, causing lumps, a greasy coat and areas of dead skin. Veterinary attention is needed to deal with it.

Ringworm – this is zoonotic and is signified by round areas of hair loss and flaky skin.

Key question
My dog is always scratching. Why?
Itchy skin can be caused by all sorts of things such as an unsuitable diet, parasite infestation, an allergy, a fungal infection, or even a reaction to shampoo/conditioners. Consult your vet to ascertain the cause so appropriate treatment can be administered.

Sneezing and vomiting

Just like humans, dogs can have bouts of sneezing, coughing or vomiting and it doesn't mean there is anything seriously wrong. However, sustained periods of any of these symptoms could be due to a viral infection, which will need veterinary treatment to treat it.

Sneezing – this can be caused by dust, pollen or other micro-particle substances affecting the nasal passages, so your dog sneezes to clear it. On the other hand, it can be caused by non-malignant polyps, or something more sinister, in the nasal passages, so if your dog sneezes a lot on a regular basis, have him examined by a vet.

Coughing – this is usually caused by 'kennel cough', which is a highly contagious respiratory disease caused by the bacterium *Bordetella*

bronchiseptica and canine parainfluenza virus, either separately or together. It isn't life-threatening but is distressing for both dog and owner. Symptoms comprise a bad, dry cough that worsens during exercise or if a dog pulls against the lead. Coughing bouts may finish with retching and sometimes mucus is produced from the mouth, plus there may be a nasal discharge and high temperature. Treatment comprises antibiotics from your vet.

Vomiting – this is a symptom of another condition and not an illness in itself. Causes are many, including a sudden change in diet, upset from scavenged food, trauma to the head, heatstroke, bacterial or viral infection, worms, or a foreign body in the stomach. Occasional vomiting is normal (usually after eating grass), but in recurring cases or where large amounts are produced, or if there is blood in the vomit, seek veterinary attention.

Lameness and stiffness

Dogs are naturally active and so their bodies experience a good deal of wear and tear throughout their lives, particularly where joints are concerned. It's therefore hardly surprising that they can become lame and stiff, and both young and older dogs alike can suffer impaired mobility.

Causes – these range from a thorn in a paw, which is easily treated, to something more serious that needs veterinary attention and the necessity of painkilling medication and diet supplementation to ease a dog's discomfort and aid his mobility.

Treatment – the first thing to do is check for broken bones, foreign objects lodged in feet, cut pads or ingrowing claws, that cause lameness, and treat appropriately. If lameness persists, then further investigation is warranted – see the table below.

COMMON CAUSES OF LAMENESS

Ailment	Symptom	Cause	Treatment
Osteoarthritis (degenerative joint disease: DJD, also known as OA)	Swollen joints, stiffness on rising and after exercise, lameness, difficulty climbing stairs, running or even walking. Yelping in pain and/or depressed demeanour	Worn joint cartilage in older dogs. Often exacerbated by obesity that puts strain on joints. Large breeds are more commonly affected	Diagnosis confirmed via X-ray. There is no cure, but restricted exercise, anti-inflammatory drugs, pain relief and weight control will help improve quality of life. Nutraceutical diet supplementation may help, as can hydrotherapy
Osteochondritis dissecans (OCD)	Gradual onset of lameness before 12 months old. Limping/stiffness worse when getting up after rest and after exercise	Joint cartilage disease of the shoulder and/or leg(s). Tends to affect younger, growing, dogs, especially large and giant breeds	Diagnosis is via X-ray. Restricted exercise, anti-inflammatory drugs, painkillers and possibly surgery. An appropriate diet change may be advised by your vet

Eye, ear and mouth problems

Your dog's eyes, ears and mouth are his gateway to the world – problems seeing, hearing and eating can cause major trouble for him, so you need to check these areas on a daily basis to ensure they are healthy and functioning normally.

Foreign objects – if you spot a grass seed or other object in the eyes or ears that you cannot gently remove with a cotton bud, take your pet to a vet. If something is stuck, or impaled, seek vet treatment urgently – never try to pull it out yourself in case you cause more damage.

Excess tears – sometimes this is due to excessive tear production being facilitated to flush out debris from the eye(s). Prolonged weepiness could be due to tear ducts being blocked, turned-in eyelids, or infection so your pet needs to be taken to the vet for diagnosis and effective treatment.

Head shaking – if prolonged, this is usually due to foreign objects in an ear, ear infection or ear mite infestation. Seek veterinary advice.

Impaired vision – failing eyesight is usually noticed if your dog starts bumping into things, can't find you easily or discolouration of the eye becomes apparent. Cloudy eyes are not necessarily a sign of blindness, but could be due to cataracts forming. Take your dog to a vet without delay.

Periodontal disease – this is where your dog suffers swollen and sore gums, a build-up of tartar on the teeth (hardened plaque) and foul-smelling breath (which can also indicate renal failure). In severe cases, mouth disease can affect appetite, cause rotten teeth and toxins from mouth or tooth infection can cause heart disease and other ailments. Consult your vet for treatment and advice on oral hygiene and a suitable diet.

Key fact

Sticks and stones can damage a dog's mouth and break teeth, so never use these as canine playthings.

The senior dog

An ageing dog can provide companionship that's just as rewarding as playing with a puppy. A 'golden oldie' may be a bit slower mentally and physically, but his affection and loyalty will be undiminished and you can do much to enable him to enjoy his autumn years with you.

The ageing process

Signs of old age creeping in are not hard to spot: your pet starts
to take things easier, spends more time sleeping and ease of
movement reduces. Dark-haired dogs become grey around the
muzzle and their hearing and eyesight may diminish.

Key fact

Old dogs can suffer from canine senile
dementia, which is the equivalent of
Alzheimer's disease in humans. Symptoms
include: irritability, abnormal sleeping
patterns and vocalization, confusion and
disorientation. Veterinary drugs are
available that can help.

SIGNS OF AGEING

Sign	Effect	Treatment
Impaired vision	Bumping into things and disorientation	Seek veterinary advice, and avoid moving furniture around
Deafness	He 'ignores' vocal commands due to him failing to hear you, or respond to noise	Seek veterinary advice in case there's a treatment; otherwise teach your dog hand signals to replace vocal commands
Stiffness	Impaired movement and pain	See pages 168–169. Orthopaedic beds can help alleviate discomfort, as can diets specifically for older dogs
Incontinence	Soiling in the house	Never chastise your pet for something he cannot help. Drug therapy may help, otherwise replace carpets with soil-proof flooring in areas your dog goes, so urine and faeces are easily cleaned up
Lack of appetite	Weight loss and lethargy	Seek veterinary advice to determine the cause and prescribe treatment for mouth ailments if necessary. If all is clear, change food to a more appetizing and easy to eat variety
Unpleasant body odour	He smells bad!	Some veterinary drugs can cause nasty body odour, as can skin ailments, overproductive oil glands, poor oral hygiene and blocked anal sacs. Consult your vet
Excessive thirst	Always drinking water and urinating more	Causes for this are usually diabetes mellitus or renal failure. Veterinary treatment is required

Health problems

As your dog ages he will need more regular healthcare and may develop some minor health problems. When your dog reaches the age of 5–7, take him for twice-yearly veterinary check-ups so that health problems can be picked up early and treated appropriately.

Key question
How do dog and human ages compare?
As an approximate guide, equate 14 human years to a dog's first year and add 7 for each following year, as follows...

Dog Years	Human Years
1	14
2	21
3	28
4	35

and so forth

Generally, smaller dogs live longer than large breeds, for example Irish Wolfhounds live for only 8–9 years, whereas a Yorkshire Terrier may still be going strong at 15.

Kidney disease – renal failure is indicated by insatiable thirst, copious urination, vomiting, diarrhoea, loss of appetite, weight loss and halitosis. Immediate veterinary attention is necessary, but survival rates are slim.

Lack of agility injuries – joint stiffening and general slowing down can result in torn ligaments, broken bones, knocks and sprains. Several gentle, slow, exercise sessions per day are better than one or two injury-inducing energetic ones.

Constipation – old dogs may not chew and digest food efficiently, which can lead to constipation, as can a lack of mobility. Choose an age-related diet that's easier for oldies to cope with, and encourage more water intake and gentle exercise.

Degenerative spinal disease – this is indicated by the gradual loss of use of the

hind legs. Your vet will advise treatment, but there is no cure and it gets worse with time.

Lumps and bumps – these should be checked out by a vet. Cancer is the biggest killer of older dogs so the sooner it is picked up the better the chances of it being treated successfully. Feel over your dog daily to check for unexplained lumps on or under the skin's surface.

Breathing difficulties – excessive panting, in an effort to draw in sufficient oxygen, can indicate a heart or lung problem.

The senior dog **177**

Senior care

An elderly dog may sit around a lot and be undemanding and quiet, but he should not be ignored. To help maintain his physical and mental fitness for as long as possible, your ageing pet needs lots of extra-special care to ensure he stays feeling good for as long as possible.

Give reassurance – old dogs are often clingier, usually because their senses are failing and they are therefore more susceptible to anxiety. Consider moving his bed into your bedroom at night to help prevent or alleviate geriatric separation anxiety (see pages 144–145).

Lifestyle – like elderly people, old dogs are resistant to and are upset by changes in their environment and routine. Incorporate any changes gradually to allow your dog to acclimatize slowly.

Exercise – if your dog has remained fit and active throughout his life, carry on exercising him as normal on the basis that 'if he doesn't use it, he will lose it'. He will tell you when he needs to slow down.

Key tip
To prevent an old dog whose eyesight and hearing isn't 100 per cent from wandering into trouble, such as on the road or becoming lost, always keep him on the lead or your eye on him when he's exercised loose in public places.

Age concern

To remain contented and in the best possible health, an elderly dog needs everything on this checklist:

- Plenty of love and affection
- Keeping warm
- Particular attention to teeth and claws
- Extra care with diet (see pages 180–181)
- Help with grooming
- Exercise dependent on his physical condition
- Patience and understanding (especially with toileting accidents)
- Twice-yearly vet checks (see pages 176–177)
- Constant daily routine
- Minimal upheaval
- Plenty of sleep

Playtime – it is still important to stimulate your elderly dog with games and toys – it will help to maintain his mental and physical fitness (see pages 182–183).

Younger generation – if you decide to get a puppy before your older dog has passed on, be aware that as the puppy matures it may issue pack hierarchy challenges over the older, weaker dog, which may make the latter's life miserable. Ensure that a newcomer ('intruder') does not receive more fuss and attention than the existing dog otherwise this could induce jealousy in the older dog, resulting in aggression between them or depression in the latter.

New companion – getting another dog, adult or puppy, to act as a replacement companion when one of a couple has died, has both pros and cons. If it works, it can give a pining, older dog a new lease of life, or it could serve to stress and frustrate him, especially if the replacement bullies or pesters him (see left). So think carefully before taking on a new companion to replace a deceased one.

Comfort – make sure your dog's bed has a warm comfortable blanket and keep him protected from cold weather with a special doggy coat. Orthopaedic beds can provide extra comfort and support to ageing dogs.

Feeding senior dogs

Complete foods especially formulated for senior dogs are widely available and these contain all the nutrients the ageing body needs to remain in the best possible condition and help delay or alleviate the onset of conditions such as senility.

Low protein – as older dogs can often suffer from liver-related problems, a diet low in protein may be applicable. Ask your vet about the best diets for older dogs.

Food defence – elderly pets may not be able to defend their food from younger dogs in the household stealing it. Feed your golden oldie separately to ensure he gets his daily quota and feels secure enough to enjoy it.

Trouble eating – this is usually due to a mouth ailment such as gum disease, tooth problems or even possibly a mouth abscess. Get your dog checked by a vet. If all is clear, try serving food at room temperature, or warm it slightly in case tooth sensitivity to cold food is causing the problem. Try also using soft, wet or semi-moist food for ease of eating (and help prevent constipation due to increased water intake), but clean teeth regularly to prevent plaque and tartar build-up.

Key fact

Chews help maintain mouth hygiene as well as keeping an older dog occupied and entertained.

Oily fish – substituting meat for tuna, pilchards or sardines in vegetable oil a couple of times a week can help prevent constipation, as well as promote healthier joints, skin and coat. These fish are also good for tempting dogs that have lost their appetite.

Weight changes – old dogs are prone to putting on weight if their mobility is compromised, but this can worsen conditions such as joint problems and heart disease. Consult your vet about an appropriate diet and what amounts to give daily. Conversely, a dog that shows signs of weight loss also requires veterinary attention to ascertain the cause.

Exercise and mental agility

An older dog is likely to tire on long walks, but as he needs to exercise to remain as physically fit as possible, to ward off obesity and keep him supple, switch to several short walks a day. Likewise, his brain needs to be kept active – and there are lots of ways in which you can do this.

Over-exercising – try to go on several, different short walks each day, so as not to physically exhaust your pet and to maintain his interest. Include short obedience training sessions and playtime on walks for additional variety.

Hydrotherapy – this is good exercise for dogs with impaired mobility since it does not tax joints. Some insurance policies cover this in event of your p... becoming infirm, so it's worth checking t...

Hide-and-seek ... daily food ration... has two-fold be...

for him to enjoy, and he'll exercise himself finding the food. You can also scatter treats around the house for him to seek out.

...n games – gentle tug games and ...ing exercises that your pet can do ...ortably – such as sit, stay, fetch and ...e a paw – will help keep life enjoyable ...ou and your dog.

Bereavement

When a dog dies, or his death is imminent, it usually has a profound effect on those humans who loved him. It does help you cope a little better with the trauma if you understand why and how it happens.

Why dogs die – this is for two reasons: sudden death through accident or illness; or euthanasia (being 'put down' or 'put to sleep') following an accident or due to illness when a cure is not possible and the dog's quality of life is, or will be, poor and/or painful.

Natural death – if death is sudden due to accident or a heart attack, it is upsetting for owners – but instant. A prolonged natural death is extremely traumatic for both dog and owner, and painful for the former.

Where? – in cases of emergency you sometimes don't have a choice, and this is usually at the vet's clinic. If you know that it is imminent, talk it over with your vet first, as to whether a home or clinic visit is best for you and your dog, and arrange a date sooner rather than later so as not to prolong your dog's suffering, as well as your own.

Euthanasia – an injection comprising a type of barbiturate (which causes the heart to

Key question
How will I know when the time is right to have my old dog euthanized?
It's time to let him go if his major organs and/or limbs begin to fail and he is unable to function without mental distress or physical pain.

stop) is given, usually into a leg vein. The process takes only seconds: during and after the injection the dog becomes drowsy, lapses into unconsciousness and dies peacefully.

Counselling – bereavement counselling is available from many canine, as well as human, charities, and it can really help to talk things over with someone who understands your grief.

Loss of a companion – if a dog is used to having a canine companion and playmate in the house, then its loss can affect the survivor

– simply by it being confused that its canine companion is no longer there. Help alleviate this by carrying on with your usual routine – the sooner things are back to normal after a pet loss, the better for remaining pets.

Remember, dogs don't have the same 'human' emotions regarding bereavement as we do, so as long as they receive their usual daily care, attention, food and exercise, they are quite happy. See page 178 for introducing new dogs.

Doggy funerals

It may not be pleasant to think about, but being prepared as to what to do after your pet's death well before this happens will make this rite of passage less stressful for you.

Home burial – many people, if they are fit and able to dig a suitably-sized, 1 metre (3 feet) deep, grave, choose to bury their dog in the garden, but you must check with your local authority to ensure you are allowed to do this. Bear in mind that this can be a difficult job if the ground is hard or frozen.

Veterinary disposal – your vet can arrange disposal of your dog's body for a fee. Dogs are usually taken to landfill (if allowed depending on where you live) or are cremated along with others. Alternatively, you can request that your pet is buried or cremated and have his ashes returned to you. Enquire what the options and costs are.

Pet cemetery – you can choose to have your pet cremated (with the ashes returned to you in a presentation casket) or buried. Check your local telephone directory for services in your area or ask your vet for advice; alternatively, search the Internet. Enquire what the service comprises and what optional extras there are, such as coffins and headstones.

Keepsakes – from commissioning a portrait of your pet, or having a 'diamond' or paperweight made from his ashes, there are a number of ways to remember him. Again, check the Internet or canine magazines for options.

Memories – remember, though, that the memories you hold in your head make the best keepsakes of all.

Going out with a bang

You can even have your pet's ashes incorporated into a firework. Some people like to do this on what would have been the dog's next birthday, or other special occasion. Check the Internet for such services.

Index

a

abnormal behaviour/signs 158, 163
ACER (Attention, Command, Execute, Reward) 114–15
adolescence 69
adulthood 69
ageing process 174–5
aggression 37, 38, 133, 140–1
allergies 15, 164
alternative therapies 145
attention-seeking 110–11
  puppies 52, 57

b

barking 36–7
bathing 82–3
bed and bedding 46–7, 179
bedtime 51
benefits of dogs 6, 10
bereavement 184–5
birth 41
bites 162
bloat 164
body language 38–9
body odour 175
body stance 37, 39
bones 22, 23
Boxers 127
brachycephalic breeds 26
breath 65, 170
breathing difficulties 177
breed characteristics 14, 142
burials 186

c

cancer 177
car journeys 50, 71, 150
cariac muscle 25
carrying dogs 12
cats 57, 77, 136
character traits 36
chase control 136–7
chewing 50, 138–9, 142
chews 139, 180
children 10, 12–13, 80
  feeding dogs at the table 112
  and 'leave' training 118
  and puppies 54
choosing a dog 14–15
circulatory system 28–9
clicker training 114
'Close!' command 103
coat 32–3
  health check 78
colds 156
collar training 75, 104
collars 46, 86
colour vision 35
'Come' command 122–3
commands
  and chase control 136–7
  'Come' 122–3
  confusion with 102
  consistency of 102
  'Down' 103 120–1
  'Heel' 106–7
  'Here' 103
  'Leave' 16, 118–19
  'No' 16
  'Over' 103
  'Sit' 103, 114–15
  'Stand' 103
  'Stay' 103, 116–17, 129
  'Watch me' 103
communication 36–7
conditioned rewards 122
constipation 164, 176, 180
coughing 156, 166–7
counselling for bereavement 184
cowering 38
crates 47, 50, 150
cremation 186
cross-breeds 14
cues (hand signals) 102, 103, 175

d

DAP (dog-appeasing pheromone) diffusers 142, 145, 147
deafness 175
death and bereavement 184–5
degenerative diseases 169, 176–7
destructive tendencies 138–9, 142
dewclaws 22
diarrhoea 164
digestive system 30–1
digging 17
disc-training 136
doorways 111
'Down' command 103, 120–1

e

ears 39, 80, 170, 171
emergencies 162, 163
euthanasia 184
eye contact 13
eyes 79, 170

f

faeces 17, 31, 47, 61, 79
family friendly breeds 15
fears and phobias 146–7
feet 22
females (bitches) 40, 66–7
   neutering 62, 63
fireworks, fear of 142, 147
first aid 162–3
fish, oily 180
flatulence 164
fleas 156
food/feeding 15, 48–9, 54, 65,
   88–97, 91
   amounts 92–3
   begging 95, 112, 113
   bowls 46
   fussy eaters 94
   hygiene 91
   leftovers 93
   natural diets 90
   nutrients 91
   older dogs 180–1
   permission to eat 101, 118
   puppies 48–9, 54, 65
   and teeth 65, 180
   and training 96–7, 101
   treats 95, 96–7
   types of food 90–1
   weight-watching 92, 95
   wet food 91
funerals 186
fungal infections 164

g

garden safety 86
geriatric separation anxiety 37,
   144, 178
German Shepherds 32, 164
Golden Retrievers 32
grass eating 30
grass-scratching 16
Great Danes 164
Greyhounds 32
grooming 12, 15, 80–1
   kit 47
guarding breeds 14
gundogs 14

h

hackles 39
hair/hairs 14–15, 32
hand signals 102, 103, 175
head shaking 170
health care/problems 135,
   154–71
   breeds 15
   colds 156
   coughing 166–7
   ears 170, 171
   eyes 170
   first aid 162–3
   fleas 156
   head shaking 170
   health checks 78–9
   lameness 168–9
   mouth problems 170
   older dogs 175, 176–9
   signs of illness 158–61
   skin problems 164
   sneezing 166
   stiffness 168–9, 175
   stomach problems 164
   TRP rates 159
   vaccinations 156
   vomiting 167
   worms 156
hearing 34
'Heel' command 106–7
herbal remedies 145
herding breeds 14
'Here' command 103
hide-and-seek 183
holidays 151
hounds 14
house rules 124–5
house safety 86
howling at night 37
hydrotherapy 183

i

identity
   permanent markers 87
   tags/discs 46, 86
impaired vision 175
incontinence 175

j

juvenile puppies 68

k

keepsakes 186
kidney disease 176

l

lameness 168–9
lead training 75, 104–5
leads 46, 108
'Leave' command 16, 118–19
licking faces 36
life stages 68–9
lips 30
liver 97
lumps 177

m

male dogs 62, 63, 66, 67
massage 84–5
mating 40
mental state 37
microchipping 87
mongrels 14
mood swings 67
motion sickness 150
mouth 30, 64–5, 79
    problems 170, 180
muscular system 24–5

n

nails 78, 80
naming 54
nervous dogs 142–3
neutering 62–3
'No' command 16
noises, fear of 142, 146, 147

o

obesity 79, 95
objects
    in eyes/ears 170
    fear of 147
    swallowing 139
oestrus 40
older dogs 172–87
    ageing process 174–5
    bereavement 184–5
    exercise and mental agility
        182–3
    feeding 180–1
    health care 178–9
    health problems 175, 176–7
    and new puppies/dogs 179
    rescuing 19
    separation anxiety 144–5
    training 126–7

walks 152, 178, 182
osteoarthritis (OA) 169
osterochondritis dissecans
    (OCD) 169
'Over' command 103

p

panic attacks 144
panting 27
pawing 39
pedigrees 15
periodontal disease 170
pet cemeteries 186
phobias 146–7
play 13, 56–7
    older dogs 179, 183
play-biting 53, 71
poisoning 163
poodles 15
poop scoops 47
possessiveness 124
praise and reward 100–1
pregnancy 40–1
problem behaviours 130–47
    reasons for 132–3
pulse rate 159
puppies 42–57
    attention-seeking 52, 57
    birth 41
    bringing home 50–1
    choosing and finding 44–5
    classes for 56
    equipment 46–7
    feeding 48–9, 54, 65
    handling 54–5
    health checks 78–9
    leaving alone 50
    life stages 68–9
    mouths and teeth 64–5
    naming 54

and older dogs 179
and other pets 57, 77
playing with 56–7
size of litter 41
socialization 71, 76–7
toileting 50, 51, 53
see also training

r

rabies 156
reproduction 40–1
rescue dogs 18–19, 129, 143
    puppies 45
respiration rate 159
respiratory system 26–7
rewards 100–1, 105, 108
    and clicker training 114
    conditioned 122
    rewarding good behaviour
        111, 113, 135
ringworm 164
road safety 77, 108–9
rolling 39

s

safety 86, 143
saliva 14–15, 30–1
scooting 17
scratching 164
seborrhoea 164
security 86–7, 143
senile dementia 37, 174
senses 34–5
separation anxiety 37, 142,
    144–5, 178
sexual maturity 66–7
shedding (moulting) 33
sight 35
'Sit' command 103, 114–15
skeletal muscles 24, 25

skeleton 22–3
skin 32, 164
smell 34
smelly breath 65, 170
'smiling' 38
sneezing 166
sniffing 37, 39
socialization 71, 76–7
    older dogs 127
Springer Spaniels 127
Stair-gates 111
'Stand' command 103
'Stay' command 103, 116–17, 129
sticks 170
stiffness 168–9, 175
stings 163
stomach problems 52, 164
stones 170

t
table manners 112–13
tail-wagging 37, 39
taste 35
tattooing 87
tears 170
teeth 30, 65
    cleaning 81, 180
    older dogs 180
    periodontal disease 170
temperature taking 159
terriers 14, 37
thirst, excessive 175
thunder, fear of 147
toilet-training 60–1, 128–9
toileting
    incontinence 175
    puppies 50, 51, 53, 79
tongue 30
touch 35

toy breeds 14
toys 47, 50–1, 53
training 98–129
    and aggressive behaviour 141
    classes 74, 124
    clicker training 114
    confusion 102, 128
    consistency in 102, 110, 128
    disc-training 136
    food for 96–7
    hand signals 102, 103
    heel training 105–7
    house manners 124–5
    lead training 75, 104–5
    learned responses 100–1
    older dogs 126–7
    plan 70–1
    praise and reward 100–1, 105
    resolving problems 128–9
    road safety 77, 108–9
    sessions 100, 127
    socialization 71, 76–7
    starting again 128
    teaching patience 110–11
    toilet-training 60–1
    working breeds 127
    see also commands
travelling 50, 71, 150–1
treats 95, 96–7
TRP (temperature, pulse and respiration) rates 159

u
unacceptable behaviour 101, 102
urine/urination 31, 79

v
vaccinations 156, 157
vegetarian diets 90
veterinary diets 90–1
vets/vet clinics 77
    emergencies 162, 163
    euthanasia 184
visceral muscles 24, 25
vision 35
voice commands in training 102–3
vomiting 167

w
walks/walking
    benefits of 10
    meeting other dogs 152
    older dogs 152, 178, 182
    poor exercise tolerance 152
    pulling 152
    puppies 71, 77
    returning when off lead 153
    safety 77, 86, 108–9
    slow walking 152
'Watch me' command 103
water 49, 91
    bowls 46
    drinking dirty 16
    safety 86
weight-watching 79, 92, 180
whiskers 33
working breeds 14, 127
worms 156
wounds 162

y
yawning 38

Acknowledgements

Executive Editor Trevor Davies

Editor Ruth Wiseall

Deputy Creative Director Karen Sawyer

Designer Mark Stevens

Picture Researcher Giulia Hetherington

Senior Production Controller Carolin Stransky

Picture credits

Alamy Ernie Janes 137; Jeremy Pardoe 154; Juniors Bildarchiv 49, 51, 130; Karon Swan 8; macana 119; Petra Wegner 95, 145; Steven May 18; VStock 144.

Angela Hampton 161.

Ardea John Daniels 40, 41.

Corbis Image Source 146.

Dorling Kindersley Steve Shott 117.

Dreamstime.com Anke Van Wyk 166.

FLPA Foto Natura Catalogue 187; Gerard Lacz 36.

Fotolia.com Callalloo Candcy 127; Igor Lokshin 148; judwick 174; Simone van den Berg 91; Waldemar D & #261; browski 2, 42.

Getty Images AFP/Liu Jin 109; Dave King/Dorling Kindersley 171; Greg Ceo 178.

Nature Picture Library Petra Wegner 7.

Octopus Publishing Group 11, 57, 64, 67, 77, 84, 86, 105, 185; Angus Murray 16 below; 46, 47 above & below, 48, 55, 60, 61, 93, 94, 96, 104, 106, 110, 114, 116, 126, 138, 139, 143, 153; Jane Burton 68; Ray Moller 15; Rosie Hyde 160,168; Russell Sadur 12, 13, 53, 72, 75, 76, 78, 79 left & right, all 81, 82-3, 84-5, 90, 113, 120, 123, 125, 128, 129, 134, 157, 163,183; Steve Gorton 1 & 115, 16 above, 17, 19, 38 above & below, 50, 52, 54, 65, 66, 101, 151, 177.

Photolibrary Group Andersen Ross 112, 165; Cusp/Simon Plant 185; Fotosearch 98; Image Source 172; Jim Craigmyle 4; Juniors Bildarchiv 20, 44, 58, 70; Oxford Scientific/Justin Paget 181.

Warren Photographic 133, 141, 167.